Kids Can!

Know God's Rules &
Rewards for Right Choices

by

Elizabeth Snyder Pearson

authorHOUSE®

AuthorHouse™
1663 Liberty Drive, Suite 200
Bloomington, IN 47403
www.authorhouse.com
Phone: 1-800-839-8640

First published by AuthorHouse   5/22/2008

ISBN: 978-1-4343-8376-1 (sc)

Library of Congress Control Number: 2008903955

Printed in the United States of America
Bloomington, Indiana

This book is printed on acid-free paper.

Theme Of This Book

"But thou, O man of God...

Follow after righteousness,

godliness, faith, love,
patience, meekness.

Fight the good fight of faith,

lay hold on eternal life...

Lay up in store for yourself

a good foundation

against the time to come...

Lay hold on eternal life."

I Timothy 6:11,12,19

Contents

Introduction 1

To Parents 2

To Boys And Girls 3

To Teens 4

To Adults 5

To Seniors 6

Parenthood 7

Children 8

Fathers 9

Mothers 10

Grandparents 11

Names 12

Obedience 13

Punishment 14

Friendships 15

Neighbors 16

Neatness 17

Consideration 18

Time 19

Laziness 20

Hygiene 21

Sharing 22

Favoritism 23

Accidents 24

Temper 25

Revenge 26

Stubbornness 27

Patience 28

Forgiving 29

Eyes 30

Looking 31

Reading 32

Television 33

Ears 34

Listening 35

Respect	36
Schoolwork	37
Mouths	38
Eating	39
Diet	40
Smile	41
Tongue	42
Lying	43
Deceit	44
Gossip	45
Promises	46
Hands	47
Dexterity	48
Writing	49
Stealing	50
Smoking	51
Drinking	52
Gambling	53
Feet	54
Heart	55
Love	56
Honesty	57
Thankfulness	58
Contentment	59
Happiness	60
Joy!	61
Jealousy	62
Selfishness	63
Giving	64
God	65
Bible	66
Truth	67
Faith	68
Works	69
Trust	70
Believing	71
Salvation	72

God's Ten Commandments 73

Church 74

Worship 75

Unity 76

Allowance 77

Tithing 78

Prayer 79

Witnessing 80

Gifts 81

Talents 82

Coveting 83

Body 84

Exercise 85

Sleep 86

Play 87

Sports 88

Competition 89

Judging 90

Popularity 91

Heroes 92

Humility 93

Minds 94

Knowledge 95

Wisdom 96

Thoughts 97

Choices 98

Priorities 99

Studying 100

Memorizing 101

Computers 102

Worry 103

Fears 104

Goals 105

Obstacles 106

Catastrophies 107

Failure 108

Sorrow 109

Illness	110
Suffering	111
Hope	112
Protection	113
Guidance	114
Future	115
Dating	116
Courting	117
Marriage	118
Commitment	119
Adultery	120
Work	121
Servants	122
Appreciation	123
America	124
Our Flag	125
Diversity	126
Holy Spirit	127
Saints	128
Idols	129
God's Will	130
Missionaries	131
Creation	132
Evolution	133
Angels	134
Satan	135
Sin	136
Temptation	137
Atheists	138
Old Age	139
Alzheimer's	140
Death	141
Funerals	142
The Rapture	143
Heaven	144
Anti-christ	145
Judgment	146

God's Agenda   147
Schedule of Future Events   148
Abstinence   151
All Of Life   152
A Toddler's Prayers   153
Prayer Project   154
Be Involved   155
Big Or Little?   156
Come Sailing With Me!   158
Comprehending God   159
Dare!   160
Don't Let Go!   161
Do We Think We Know It All?   162
Dumping!   164
I Don't Want A 'Grumpy' Grandma!   165
I Ran Away From Home!   166
Luxuries   167
Marriage Is Forever   168
My Car   169
My Prayer   170
My Riches   171
Night Light   172
Paying Attention   173
Prayer Is...   175
Race Track   176
Self Defense   177
Serving   178
Showing Love   179
Submission   180
Success   181
The Effects of TV   183
The Five-fingered Prayer   184
The Marathon Of Life   186
What God Wants You To Know   187
Who Deserves The Glory?   188
Our Family Prayer   189
Epilogue   190

Introduction

Parents must begin early to implant Christian values
into the lives of their children. Young people
need to know HOW God would have them
live their lives in this present world,
where temptations and self-centeredness
abounds.

The poems contained herein are short and in
language they can understand. If the words
cannot be mastered, an adult should assist
and be on hand to discuss and/or explain the issue.

This book is organized to reach children, teens,
adults and oldsters. Parents should decide when
to introduce a subject -- perhaps when a specific
situation arises that a poem addresses.
Bible references are given for God's emphasis.
Young people should be alerted that they can
refer to the book all through their lifetime.

Scripture is included for each subject and
parent and child, young adult or oldster
should look them up, study their admonition
from the Lord and seek to follow what He
prescribes. Of course, the verses included
do not completely cover everywhere such
instruction is given in the Bible.
You may find many others!

To Parents

I am of the opinion that Sunday School lessons repeat
Bible stories, with a little more emphasis through the years
on how to love Jesus and each other and to tell their
friends about Him.

However, in this day and age, when kids are exposed to
so much in their daily lives, it is my conviction that,
at an earlier age, we can help them to
understand what being a Christian is all about...
not just loving God and others alone.

I hope you will agree that kids need to know of
FUTURE EVENTS
in God's Timetable...what the world is all about and
what God's plan is for them personally.

Do they know that Jesus is coming back again?...
that He is coming for them?!
that it is important that they live each day for Him...
to know God's Word and obey it...
to seek His will
and build for future reward in Heaven...
that they will never be judged for their sins...
that it is important how they live their lives each day --
to seek His will and build for future reward in Heaven...
how they will never be judged for their sins
but only for how well they served God.

If these truths are introduced early and adequately
explained in simple manner, I feel it will make a great
difference in the goals they set for home, school,
play, leisure, marriage, occupations and --
ALL OF LIFE!

To Boys And Girls

If God gave you wonderful parents
To love and care for you,
You should try through every day
To please them in all you do.

They work so hard to pay the bills,
To give you everything you need.
Try your best to love them back,
Their instruction to always heed (obey).

Some children in other lands
Become "orphans" with no mom or dad.
If you have two loving parents,
You should be extremely glad!

And God is your Heavenly Father.
He watches over you, too...
To help and guide you every day --
So, please Him in all you do!

To Teens

Teen life may be very hard for you, as you go through
many facets of your life --
new experiences, surroundings, choices.
You have many unanswered questions, new circles
of friends and acquaintances, new feelings.
You are seeking to be more independent --
to take more control of your life. You may struggle
to do what's right and perhaps become disappointed
in people you like and trust.

Developing into a young man or woman brings
changes that you have not expected, wanted or like,
especially if you have had no-one to explain what
these might be. But be assured they happen to all --
you are not alone in your uncertainty --
and they will come to an end! This is a transitional
period in your life. It may be hard to be patient
in waiting for your body to mature but you will gradually
become adjusted and begin again to like yourself.
You will again place trust in your parents and others.

Or, you may be one who sails through this period of life
without any fears or un-surmountable challenges.
You have a lot of parental support, stable friends
who are not stressed out about their body changes.
If you will go to the God Who made you with any and
all your frustrations -- and/or victories -- you can be
assured of His daily help. His peace and joy
will accompany you all through your teen years!!

To Adults

You have reached the realm of maturity!
You should "know it all" by now -- having survived
your teen years and are now either college-bound,
working, married and/or raising a family --
you know what you want in life and what
your goals are. You have succeeded in reaching
adulthood -- but have you succeeded in any or all
of the above scenarios? Either things are going your way
OR
are you finding your days miserable and unhappy?
How do you rate your life on a scale of 1-10?
Have things gone right or wrong?

ൟ

How are you measuring your successes or losses?
By worldly standards or by God's Word?
Are you trusting in the right things -- possessions
and wealth or on Christ's approval and blessing on
your life? Are you walking daily with Him as your Guide,
listening and heeding His Word by obeying
His commands, experiencing His love,
joy and peace?
You should be a blessing to others, building treasure
in Heaven, looking for the Lord's return, serving Him
to the best of your ability with His help.
Mature years can be
happy and fulfilling! Build your treasure in Heaven,
where no-one can take it away!
God know your needs -- and cares!

To Seniors

Some say that "old age" is no fun! And you may be one
to agree or disagree.
Yes, with added years come aches and pains you
never knew before – graying and/or loss of hair,
maybe loss of teeth, wearing a bridge or two,
pains in your joints, stomach problems,
a bad heart, periods of hot and cold --
you name it. No fun!!

Or, perhaps you have reached a ripe old age with few
or none of these maladies. But you are not as active
as before -- people in your life have come and gone --
you experience loneliness and/or depression.
You are not invited to many special occasions.
You may have been blessed with a loving family
or spend hours reflecting on good times of the past.

Whatever your situation, you need the Lord!!
He is your constant companion but you must not
neglect Him! Spend hours in fellowship.
He knows your every need -- and cares!
He gives you peace and joy despite your difficulties.
Do not neglect this One Who is always available!
Your life still counts for eternity.
Be sure to strive for God's approval and blessing.

Parenthood

If God blesses you with children,
Whether a boy or girl or more!
Don't consider them a burden,
Unwanted addition to your chores --

They are a product of your love.
God grants them as a gift --
They should bring you untold joy,
The level of your love to lift!

They are precious in His sight
And your duty is to train --
To instill in them what's right and good --
From wrongful deeds to refrain.

You are their prime example,
To model God above.
If you are steadfast and faithful,
They will know God's Fatherly love.

"That the generation to come might know them, even
the children which should be born: who should
arise and declare them to their children: that they
might set their hope on God; and not forget the
works of God, but keep his commandments."
Psalm 78:6,7; "But the mercy of the Lord is from
everlasting to everlasting to them that fear Him,
and his righteousness unto children's children."
Psalm 103:17

Psalm 36:7; Proverbs 10:1; 13:22a; 17:6;
Matthew 9:14; Mark 9:37;
Luke 11:13; 18:16

Children

Children are precious to their parents,
endowed with many a unique trait.
And, through the years we care for them.
Their successes in life we await.

We watch them stumble, perhaps fall,
as they learn to walk aright.
And Godly examples seek to be
so our offspring may reach great height.

We train, exhort and punish, too --
but their choices are their own.
Parents cannot decide their future
or control them when they're grown!

God's children, too, are precious to Him,
and each has talents unique.
He lovingly tends to all their needs,
desiring that His best they will seek.

He wrote wise guidelines in His Word.
Like His Son, to pattern their lives.
He trains, exhorts and punishes, too,
all those who in selfishness strive.

God does not force, but allows free choice.
He desires that we would do our best.
Having experienced His blessings and love,
as His children, can we do anything less?

If we have learned his precepts and obey,
To our children, we can pass them along.
If they learn at our knees how to serve the Lord,
He will lovingly protect them from all wrong.

Fathers

Your dad is very special!
He loves you with all his heart --
Ever since you were a baby,
Right from the very start.

He watches over you as you grow.
He'll teach you what you need to know.
He'll love and protect you, too,
So that no-one can be hurtful to you.

God knows that you need a dad
To show you how HE loves you,
Early in life you will see
That God is your loving father, too!

The child's response:

I'm so glad that I belong
Because my dad is big and strong!
Nothing causes me alarm
For he protects me from all harm.
Every day I will obey
And to God, for him, I'll pray!

Mothers

Your mom is very special.
She loves you with all her heart!
She prays that you will love her back
And always try to do your part.

To keep home happy every day,
Try not to grumble, but obey --
If you do chores willingly,
Mother's smiles you will see.

A happy child is what mom needs
And for this she daily prays --
You'll surely want to please her
And hear her words of praise!

The child's response:

Mother loves me, this I know.
For she often tells me so.
Every day she cares for me,
Helping me God's love to see.
So I will love her in return
And all her love I'll try to earn.

Grandparents

Did you know your grandparents

Are your parents' mom and dad?

They raised your mother when she was a little girl

And your father when he was a lad.

You will find they are very special

For they love you more than you know!

They always want the best for you

And watch with pride as you grow.

So try to never disappoint them --

Try to imitate the good things you observe.

I'm sure you will do all you can to

Give the love and respect they deserve.

"Cast me not off in the time of old age; forsake me not
when my strength fails." Psalm 13:1a
"A wise son hears his father's instruction…"
Proverbs 13:1a

Job 15:10; II Timothy 1:5; Hebrews 5:14b

***See "Dumping"
"I Don't Want a Grumpy Grandma!"

Names

Parents have to name their children
And names they like they will choose --
Hoping their child will bring them honor
And not good reputation lose.

You may be named after mom or dad --
A favorite uncle, aunt or friend.
Be careful how you live each day.
Negative (bad) messages do not send!

For people will be judging you
By what you do and say --
But you have Someone to help you
If you trust in God and pray.

You do not want to dishonor
The name of your mother and dad,
But if you're careful to honor God,
Your name will never be bad!

"A good name is rather to be chosen than great riches..."
Proverbs 22:1; "A good name is better than
precious ointment." Ecclesiastes 7:1; "And whatever
ye do in word or deed, do all in the name of the Lord
Jesus..." Colossians 3:17

Psalm 28:4a; Isaiah 43:1b,7; 45:3; Jeremiah 15:16;
Luke 23:41b; Acts 7:22b; Romans 2:6

Obedience

When mom or dad calls you

To do a certain task

And you don't really feel

Like doing what they ask,

Think of all the fussing

And fuming you will save,

And just how good you'll feel

If you decide to behave.

"Do all things without murmuring" --

That means to quickly obey.

If you honor your parents,

You'll be walking in God's way.

"Children, obey your parents in the Lord;
for this is right." Ephesians 6:1
"Children, obey your parents in all things, for
this is well pleasing unto the Lord." Colossians 3:20

Psalm 37:3a, Philippians 2:14; James 1:22a

Punishment

Should you be punished when you do
something wrong?
God says that your parents can...
He has instructed them to teach you
how to behave.
To grow up an honorable woman or man!
(one who does right)

Your parents have lived for many years...
And have experienced (done) many things.
They have learned what is right and wrong
And the sad things disobedience brings.

If they are loving and serving God as they should,
They will know what is best for you!
And if you want to put Him first in your life,
You must honor all they tell you to do.

You may never have to be punished!
If you make up your mind to obey.
You will find it is far, far better
To honor what mom and dad say.

"Correct thy son, and he shall give thee rest; yes,
he shall give delight unto thy soul." Proverbs 29:17;
"...we have had fathers of our flesh which corrected
us, and we gave them reverence..." Hebrews 12:9;
"Withhold not correction from the child..." Proverbs 23:13

Hosea 4:9b

Friendships

If your friend hurts you

And you feel you want to fight --

Remember that <u>two</u> wrongs

Never make a right!

Instead of being mean to him,

Be extra nice -- in the end

You will find that he will be

An even better friend.

❧

A friend loves at all times" Proverbs 17:17a
"A man that has friends must show himself
friendly..." Proverbs 18:24a

❧

Proverbs 17:9; Luke 6:27,28; Romans 14:10

Neighbors

Do you have cranky neighbors?

Ones that seem so very sour?

How do you think you can change this?

Yes, it's within your power...

Try to be extra friendly.

Offer to help in some way...

Mow the lawn, rake the leaves,

Be kind in all that you say.

Perhaps you can run an errand,

Take the paper to their door...

You will find they are not so bad...

I'm sure you have ideas galore!

"Even a child is known by his doings, whether it be
pure, and whether it be right." Proverbs 20:11
"You should love thy neighbor as thyself." Matthew 19:19b
"Therefore all things whatsoever you would that men
should do to you, do you even so to them." Matthew 7:12a

Proverbs 14:21a, Isaiah 41:6a, Zechariah 8:16b,17a
Mark 12:31b, Luke 10:27, Romans 13:9e,10a,
Galatians 5:14, Ephesians 4:25, James 2:8

Neatness

Are you sloppy or are you neat?

Do others have to pick up after you?

Does someone have to pick up your clothes?

Is this something you make mother do?

Do you straighten the covers on your bed?

Do you pick up papers from the floor?

Are your shoes neat in your closet?

Do you rate an A+ or "poor?"

You are part of your family

And you must do your part

Or your room will always be messy --

Today I hope you will start.

❧❧

"Let all things be done decently and in order."
I Corinthians 14:40
"As you would have men do to you, do ye also
to them..." Matthew 7:12

❧❧

Psalm 51:10; Romans 7:19, 12:1;
Colossians 3:17; Hebrews 10:24

***See: "Dumping"
"I Don't Want a Grumpy Grandma"

Consideration

How comfortable are you with messes?
You say, they don't bother you?

But you are not alone in this world!
You must think of how others view…

Your room, your clothes and your hair --
even how you eat!

I think you will have many more friends
If they see you are trying to be neat.

Your schoolwork, your chores,
Your bedroom, your clothes –

Are things that many people see
So it should not be "Anything goes!"

You must not be thinking of yourself alone,
Not caring that you make other people groan!

"All things whatsoever you would that men do to you,
do ye even so to them." Matthew 7:12a
"Create in me a clean heart, O God; and renew
a right spirit within me." Psalm 51:10

Romans 12:1; I Corinthians 10:31b; 14:40,
Colossians 3:17, Hebrews 10:24

Time

Hickory, Dickory, Dock --

It's good to keep track of the time.

You should always watch the clock

So you will never get behind.

You must try to never be late

And make others wait for you...

Make good use of every minute,

Get your work in when it is due.

All have the same number of minutes

But no one uses them the same.

If you make your day count for God,

You will never be ashamed.

"My times are in thy hand." Psalms 31:15a
"Watch therefore, for ye know not what hour
your Lord doth come." Matthew 24:42

Daniel 6:10b, Matthew 24:44;
I Corinthians 10:31, II Corinthians 6:2b,
Ephesians 5:15,16

Laziness

Do you always do your part?
Not making others do your share?
You will not have many friends
If not trying your best to be fair.

Always put forth your very best effort (try)
And you will never be ashamed (feel bad),
And certainly, if you do your best,
For shirking you'll never be blamed.
(not trying)

Please think twice, if you really think
That things will just "happen" for you,
God warns that laziness brings distress –
(nothing good)
You must "rise up early" and do!

It is always easier when two do the work
Than if one must do it all alone.
You'll both feel oh, so much better
And be surprised how time has flown.

God loves the one who does his best,
Always willing to do his part...
For God did His very best for you --
The gift of His Son from His heart!

❧

"Let every man prove his own work..." Galatians 6:4
"Bear ye one another's burdens." Galatians 6:2a

Proverbs 19:15; 24:30-34; Ecclesiastes 9:10a;
Galatians 6:5; II Thessalonians 3:10b,11

Hygiene

How should you take care of yourself?
What should be your daily routine? (plan)

To make sure others around you
Like the person they're now seeing?

You must keep your body clean and neat,
Not dirty, smelly or unkempt. (messy)

Daily brush your teeth, wash your hands and face,
Better yet, a nice bath or shower take.

Make sure your clothes are not ragged or torn
But washed, ironed and colors matching...

Try not to "call attention" to yourself --
With bad habits, like itching and scratching!

Get plenty of sleep but not too much,
Get the right amount of exercise --

To do all this takes a bit of your time
But the results will greatly surprise.

People will not hesitate to have you around --
And friends of all ages will abound (be many).

❧❧

"...know ye not that your body is the temple of the Holy
Ghost which is in you...therefore glorify God in your
body and in your spirit...which are God's."
I Corinthians 6:19a,20b

❧❧

Psalm 18:20; 51:10

Sharing

All you have was given to you

So you must not selfish be,

You must be willing to share

With all those in need that you see.

You will find your heart to be glad!

And the one you have helped, as well.

Don't do it to be congratulated --

To make everyone think you are "swell!"

Do it because you love God

And thank Him for loving you.

Then those with whom you share

Will be thankful to God, too!

"Every man according as he purposes in his heart,
so let him give; not grudgingly, or of necessity:
for God loves a cheerful giver." 2 Corinthians 9:7

Proverbs 21:26b, 25:21,22; 28:27a,
Romans 12:8b

Favoritism

Be careful not to play "favorites" --
Choosing one friend over another.

Treat all as you want them to treat you
And their friendship you will not smother!
(wipe out)

Make as many friends as you can ---
Avoid causing competition or strife.

You'll find that all through the years
Friends will bring great joy to your life.

As a friend, you can also help others --
As an example of faithfulness and love.

For all are precious souls to God --
Be an example of your Father above.

"You should not respect persons." Deuteronomy 16:19b
"For there is no respect of persons with God."
Romans 2:11

Proverbs 28:21a; James 2;9a

Accidents

Sometimes you'll do something wrong

And you really couldn't help it!

Quickly ask for forgiveness

Even when hard to admit.

Some accidents are your fault.

There are others that just happen.

Promise to be more careful

And try not to do it again.

Every accident should remind you

That more careful you should be.

Not rushing or trying to "save time" --

Doing each task carefully.

"He who covers his sins shall not prosper, but whoever confesses and forsakes them shall have mercy." Proverbs 28:13; "But when they in their trouble did turn unto the Lord God...and sought him, he was found of them." II Chronicles 15:4

Psalm 37:39; 46:1; 50:15; 86:7; 91:15;
Luke 6:17c; Ephesians 4:32

Temper

There's something you must never lose!

You always hurt someone when you do...

Your temper you must try to control

For, if you don't, it will control you!

When you say those angry words

You cannot take them back!

So, if you're angry, first think twice

Before you accuse or attack.

Kind words are like a medicine

They can mend the hurt and heal.

But mean words cut and make a wound

That both of you will feel!

"He who is slow to wrath is of great understanding..."
Proverbs 14:29a; "A soft answer turns away
wrath: but grievous words stir up anger." Proverbs 15:1

Proverbs 16:32; Ephesians 4:26;
I Thessalonians 4:11a

Revenge

Is it wise to try to "get even?"
When you think someone has done you wrong?

No, you must try to hold back your temper --
Do your best to get along.

You will be surprised, if you don't become angry
And say or do things you should not,

How that person will wonder why you're so nice --
And marvel at the patience you've got!

One does not win friends by throwing stones
But by giving them candy or flowers --

Kindness never backfires --
Saves you many angry hours!

So, determine to let the Lord be your judge
For He will always decide what is right...
When others take advantage of you,
Decide in your heart not to fight!

"Say not, I will do so to him as he hath done to me:
I will render to the man according to his work."
Proverbs 24:29; "...under His wings shall you
trust: his truth shall be thy shield and buckler"
Psalm 91:4

Psalm 9:4; Micah 6:8, John 8:50

***See: "Self Defense"

Stubbornness

Are you "easy-going" or stubborn?
Do you always want your own way?
You must learn to put others first
And for a spirit of kindness pray.

A mule is a "stubborn" animal --
If he wants to, he will not budge (move)!
He "stands his ground" no matter what --
(won't give in)
And you may be like that with a grudge.
(something you don't like)

If indeed, you are the only one right --
Humble and kind you must be.
Your pride must not conquer you,
Let people your Christian testimony see.

"I will behave myself wisely in a perfect way..."
Psalm 101:2a; "...pride, and arrogancy...and the
froward mouth, do I hate." Proverbs 8:13; "He that
refuses reproof errs." Proverbs 10:17b; The way
of a fool is right in his own eyes: but he that
hearkens unto counsel is wise." Proverbs 12:15;
"The way of the just is uprightness..." Isaiah 26:7a

Judges 2:19b; Psalm 25:12; 21a; 86;11a;
119:9; 143:8b; Proverbs 21:2

Patience

Do you usually do things "in a hurry"
And mistakes you usually make?
Well, slow down! To do things right --
Patience is what it takes!

Patience means to take your time,
Not to hurry just to get done.
You'll probably have to do it over
And that is never any fun!

But patience also means to be slow
To get angry with someone.
There usually is a reason
Why they've done what they have done!

You must be careful to be kind
And slow to judge their intent (reason),
You would not like to be accused --
Not be able to explain what you meant!

Patience is being slow to judge --
To show kindness and respect.
To control your anger or dislike
And not a barrier erect! (build)

❧❧

"Strengthened with all might...unto all patience
and longsuffering with joy" Colossians 1:11
"...follow after righteousness, godliness, faith, love,
patience, meekness." I Timothy 6:11b

❧❧

Nehemiah 9:17c; Proverbs 16:32;
Luke 8:15c; Romans 5:3b,4a; James 1:4

❧ 28 ❧

Forgiving

When you've done something wrong,
And are sorry for your deed (action),
You must admit that you messed up
And God's admonition (warning) heed.

First, seek forgiveness from the Lord.
And then from the hurt one, too.
God says that if you forgive,
Then He will surely forgive you!

And, if it's a friend or loved one,
(And enemies do count, too!)
That does something wrong against you --
Why, you know, don't you, what you have to do?

Never hurt someone on purpose,
Or cause them needless pain --
For even if you seem to win,
Satisfaction (a good feeling) you'll never
really gain (have).

"Blessed is he whose transgression (sin) is forgiven,
whose sin is covered." Psalm 32:1;
"Be ye angry, and sin not: let not the sun go down
upon your wrath. Neither give place to the devil."
Ephesians 4:26,27; "If we say that we have not sinned,
we make him a liar, and His word is not
in us." I John 1:8

Matthew 6:14,15; 18:21,22,35; Mark 11:25,26;
Luke 6:37;11:4; 17:3; II Corinthians 2:10; I John 1:9
11:4, 17:3

*** SEE: "ALL OF LIFE"

Eyes

What a wonderful gift!
God has given you two eyes --
If you're careful what you look at,
You will prove to be very wise.

Of course, everyone enjoys
Animals and plants to see --
And clouds in the blue, blue sky
Or giant waves in the sea!

It would be hard to be blind --
Not to see your parents' faces
Or where to take your next step,
Even to tie your shoelaces.

But God is not pleased at all
When our eyes look on things that are bad --
Like killing in computer games --
It makes the Lord very sad.

To look at sexy pictures
And read stories with swear words --
Well, I think you already know:
"That's just for all the nerds!"

❧

"I will set no wicked thing before my eyes."
Psalm 101:3a; "Mine eyes are ever toward
the Lord." Psalm 25:15a

❧

Isaiah 45:22

Looking

What you see and read and watch
Is what you learn each day.

So be careful what you look at.
In your mind it all will stay!

You do not have an eraser
To get rid of everything bad --

It's like things are written in ink
On a blank paper pad.

Your eyes are like a camera
Taking pictures all the time!

You have to decide what's good,
Refusing what is "grime." (bad)

Be careful what you read
And what you watch on TV

And if you read your Bible,
You'll learn the things to flee! (run away from)

❧❧

"I will set no wicked thing before my eyes..." Psalm 101:3a,
"Look unto me, and be ye saved, for I am God and
there is none else." Isaiah 45:22,
Isaiah 45:22

Reading

You learn a lot from your parents,
From grandmas and grandpas, too,

You'll go to school for many years
And have teachers quite a few!

But its up to you how much you will learn.
Your knowledge you <u>can</u> increase

By doing something entirely on your own --
Don't let your inquisitiveness (curiosity) cease! (stop)

Grab a book and don't let it go --
Investigate all subjects of interest to you.

So many facts and figures you'll know
to help you as you live your life through.

❧❧

"Philip... said, Do you understand what you are reading?
And he said, How can I except some man
should guide me?..." Acts 8:30b,31a
"Baruch...(read) in the book the words of Jeremiah
in the house of the Lord." Jeremiah 36:10

❧❧

II Corinthians 3:2; Ephesians 3:4; I Timothy 4:13

***SEE: "I RAN AWAY FROM HOME"
"COME SAILING WITH ME"

Television

Are you glued to the television screen?

There are programs you just HAVE to see?

Do you know how much time you spend --

How much time you have left that's free?

Be sure to get homework done first,

And your chores you must not neglect (put off).

Do you play outside and get fresh air

And your parents' wishes respect?

The best you can do is read a lot,

For that's how you learn the most.

Or work on a special project --

Of your talent then you can boast.

"I will set no wicked thing before my eyes." Psalm 101:3a;
"The eyes of the Lord are in every place, beholding
the evil and the good." Proverbs 15:3

Psalms 34:15a; Proverbs 5:21; 7:2; Matthew 26:41;
Ephesians 6:1,2, 11,12; Philippians 4:8; Colossians 3:2
I Peter 3:12a

***See "The Effects of TV"

Ears

God created your ears for hearing

But who do you listen to?

The advice of your teachers and parents

Or what your friends want you to do?

Do you listen to good music

With words you can understand?

Is the music loud and annoying?

Played by a non-Christian band?

Do the lyrics (words) honor our God above

Or do they speak of Satanic things?

You must choose stations or TV shows

That true satisfaction brings.

❧❧

"Hear counsel, and receive instruction, that thou mayest
be wise in thy latter end." Proverbs 19:20;
"Give ear…to my law: incline your ears to the words
of my mouth." Psalm 78:1

❧❧

Deuteronomy 5:27a; Psalm ll5:6a;
Matthew 11:15; 13:16

Listening

Did you know that when YOU talk
You only say what you already know?

But when you listen, and listen well,
You can learn NEW things and grow?

So don't always be yak-yakking!
Pay attention at home and at school.

And your friends, too, will appreciate
When you make them feel "really cool."

You will find you will have many friends
If you listen to what THEY have to say,

So make them feel important --
Don't always be jabbering away!

"Study to be quiet, and to do your own business..."
I Thessalonians 4:11a; "Hear instruction, and be wise,
and refuse it not." Proverbs 8:33; "Apply your heart
unto instruction, and your ears to the words of
knowledge." Proverbs 23:12

Psalm 78:1; Ecclesiastes 5:2a,
Ezekiel 40:4a; Matthew 11:15

Respect

Do you listen when others are speaking?
Do you pay attention in school?

Do you criticize others or constantly complain?
Are you careful to obey every rule?

Respect is doing what you want
Others to give to you!

So give to everyone else
All the respect that is due.

Especially to those who are older
Who, through experience, are wise,

And, yes, even to all of your friends
Regardless of age or size!

You will find that if you do this,
You'll be treated just as kind.

People will look up to you
And THEIR respect you will find.

❧

"In all things show thyself a pattern of good
works..." Titus 2:7a,8; "Honor all men.
Love the brotherhood..." I Peter 2:17a,b

❧

Psalm 119:15,17b; Luke 6:31,33,35;
Acts 10:34b; Galatians 5:13c; Ephesians 6:9c;
Colossians 3:13,25

***See "Paying Attention"

Schoolwork

Just as important as parents
Are the teachers at your school.
Be sure to be very courteous
And try to obey ev'ry rule.

Listen carefully to each lesson,
Answer whenever you can,
Be sure to do your homework,
Don't be afraid to raise your hand.

Be sure to study for a test
And never, ever cheat!
Do not whisper or disturb,
Ask permission to leave your seat.

Try to do a little "extra" -
Don't settle for a "C,"
You will find if you work real hard,
How happy you will be!

"Whosoever loveth instruction loveth knowledge..."
Proverbs 12:1a; "Even a child is known by his doings,
whether his work be pure, and whether it be
right." Proverbs 20:11; "Study to show thyself
approved unto God, a workman that needeth not
to be ashamed..." II Timothy 2:15a,b

Psalm 90:12b;

Mouths

When you hear someone arguing,

Don't you want to close your ears?

Did you know that when you say something cruel,

You can make someone burst into tears?

God says that the tongue is hard to control

And it's hard for everyone!

But you must try to keep your words clean

And of others not to make fun.

You should not boast or use foul words –

What grownups would call "swearing"

Try always to be thoughtful and kind

And to all you meet be caring.

❧

"Keep your tongue from evil, and your lips from
speaking guile (evil)." Psalm 34:13
"I said, I will take heed to my ways, that I sin not
with my tongue." Psalm 39:1

❧

Psalm 49:3; 119:29a; Proverbs 10:20; 15:4;
16:24; 21:23; Philippians 1:27a; James 3:2; 4:11a

Eating

Have you often heard your mother say,
"You must finish what's on your plate?
If there's something like "yucky" spinach --
This admonition (advice) you'll probably hate!

But when you think of those who starve
In your land and across the sea --

You must try not to waste any good food
But eat what you're served thankfully.

Be careful not to eat too little
So your body cannot healthy grow.

But don't overeat or eat too fast
For "extra" weight is not good, you know.

So, what you eat is up to you --
A balanced diet your goal should be
For then your weight will be just right
And a long, happy life you will see.

"Whether therefore ye eat, or drink, or whatever
you do, do all to the glory of God." I Corinthians 10:31

Matthew 6:25,26; Luke 12:29-31; Acts 2:46

Diet

Should you always have an extra helping?
Eat everything on your plate?
The first may help to make you fat!
The second is a good trait.

But don't take more than you can eat --
You must not wasteful be!

Just think of all those starving
In America and across the sea!

Eat enough to give you strength
To study and to play --
Lots of fruit and vegetables,
And a few treats are OK.

Always compliment mother
Or you may see her shed a tear!

Would you like to cook and bake
Each and every day of the year?!

"Know ye not that your body is the temple of the Holy
Ghost, which is in you...ye are not your own?
For ye are bought with a price: therefore glorify God
in your body, and in your spirit, which are God's.
I Corinthians 6:19,20

I Corinthians 6:12; II Peter 1:6

***See "Luxuries"

Smile

Are you a "grumpy" boy or girl

And a smile you hardly ever wear?

Are you found frowning a lot

And look like a growling bear?

Cheer up! Things are not so bad

And you will find, it's true

That, when you turn up the corners
of your mouth,

Someone else will smile at you!

A smile is a gift you can always give --

It doesn't cost you a thing!

But it shows that you are happy

And you'll make other people sing.

"Be glad in the Lord, and rejoice...Psalm 32:11
"A merry heart makes a cheerful countenance.."
Proverbs 15:13a
Psalm 9:2; 144:15b; 146:5; Proverbs 16:20b; 17:22a

Tongue

The tongue can comfort or it can burn.
This is the lesson you must learn.

It can be used for good or bad,
Make someone happy or very sad.

Don't use words that are nasty --
Or mean -- or called "swearing" --

Make them complimentary (nice)
And full of love and caring.

A kind word makes one smile
And feel really good inside --

When you're careful what you say,
You never have to run and hide!

Folks will listen if you're nice
And you'll need not have to say things twice!

❧❧❧

"...every tongue should confess that Jesus Christ is Lord..."
Philippians 2:11; "Even so the tongue is a little member...
behold, how great a matter a little fire kindles.
The tongue is a fire, a world of iniquity." James 3:5,6;
"...let us not love in word, neither in tongue; but
in deed and in truth." I John 3:18b

❧❧❧

Philippians 2:11; James 1:26; I Peter 3:10;
I John 3:18

Lying

If you lie, you're "not telling the truth!"
Which God warns us not to do!
We know that our God CANNOT lie --
This is His Pattern for you.

Lying is never acceptable (right).
It always gets you in trouble.
Instead of getting you "off the hook" --
It makes the bad to double!

If you tell the truth, how good you'll feel.
You won't have to worry or fret --
No-one can accuse you of doing wrong
And God's help and blessing you'll get!

One of God's Ten Commandments: "You should not
bear false witness against thy neighbor." Exodus 20:16;
"A faithful witness will not lie..." Proverbs 14:5; "...it was
impossible for God to lie..." Hebrews 6:18b

Acts 5:3a; Romans 1:25; 9:1; Galatians 1:20

Deceit

"Deceit" is an act of misleading.
The "whole truth" you are not telling...
It is a trick that brings you gain (success),
But you will find your friends rebelling.
(not liking you)

No-one likes such "dirty tricks"
And good friends you may soon lose.
You must be honest with everyone --
Or other companions (friends) they'll choose.

And telling "white lies" will get you in trouble,
Most tricks will often backfire!
You do not gain by being dishonest...
You will soon be known as a "liar!"

You are always safe when telling the truth
For then your friends will not mistrust you --
And friends are what you want to have --
Who know they can really trust in you.

"My lips shall not speak wickedness, nor my tongue
utter deceit." Job 27:4; "Deceit is in the heart of them
that imagine evil..." Proverbs 12:20; "...neither was
any deceit in his mouth..." (Christ) Isaiah 53:9;
"The heart is deceitful above all things, and desperately
wicked." Jeremiah 17:9; "Deliver my soul, O Lord,
from lying lips and from a deceitful tongue." Psalm 120:2

Psalm 101:7; Romans 3:13; Hebrews 3:13

Gossip

Did you say something about someone
And you know it wasn't true?
Did others then believe it?
Was it the Lord that prompted (made) you?

No, maybe you were jealous
Or wanted just to make fun --
But you really, deeply hurt that person
And the awful deed is done!

Yes, thoughtless words cause much pain.
(words said before you really think)
You can never "take them back!"
No-one feels better when they are said
So you have had nothing good to gain!

Be careful to ask forgiveness.
Pray to never say words that harm (hurt).
You will lose good friends if you do --
They'll lose all their respect (good
feelings) for you!

"Let the words of my mouth...be acceptable in thy sight,
O Lord..." Psalm 19:14; "...the words of the pure
are pleasant words." Proverbs 15:26; "He that hath
knowledge spares his words..." Proverbs 17:27a;
"...the words of a talebearer are as wounds..."
Proverbs 18:8; "He that covers a transgression
seeks love; but he that repeats a matter
separates friends." Proverbs 17:9

Psalm 36:3; 55:21; Proverbs 6:2; 15:1; 26:22a;
I Timothy 1:13; II Timothy 2:14; III John 10b

Promises

It is very important --
All the choices that you make!

Think twice when making a promise
For it's something you should not break.

I'm sure you do not like it much
When someone changes their mind --
To satisfy their own desires
And ignore yours is unkind!

Words are very important
You must always mean what you say!

Try to think carefully first --
And it always helps to pray!

❦❦

"Hear, for I will speak of excellent things and the
opening of my lips shall be right things." Proverbs 8:6b
"Choose you this day whom you will serve...but as
for me and my house, we will serve the Lord."
Joshua 24:15a,c

❦❦

Deuteronomy 5:27b; Psalm 49:3; 119:172

Hands

God has given you two hands.
With them, what can you do?
Draw or play an instrument?
Be an expert at barbecue?

Take your frisky dog for a walk?
Feed your kitten its daily meals?
Help your mom set the table --
Maybe the carrots you can peel?

Take the neighbor his newspaper?
Rake the leaves or run to the store?
Take out the garbage, make your bed?
I know you'll think of many more!

Keep your hands busy doing good.
Use the talents (things you do well)
that God has given you.
Be thankful your wrist and fingers work --
Find many good things to do!

"The Lord rewarded me according to my righteousness;
according to the cleanliness of my hands…"
Psalm 18:20; "…whatsoever ye do in word or deed,
do all in the name of the Lord Jesus…" Colossians 3:17,
"…and whatsoever ye do, do it heartily, as to the Lord,
and not unto men." Colossians 3:23

Psalm 18:20; 119:48; I Timothy 2:8a

Dexterity
(Skill)

Your hands are very amazing!

They do what your mind says to do...

They can play the piano, clarinet or guitar --

And make something old look new.

They can throw a ball and swing a bat,

They can even cook on the grill.

They can write and draw and even type.

And when you are sick, give you a pill!

They can also pick up a book, good or bad,

Steal, hurt or help someone.

You must always use your hands for good --

A musician or doctor you may become!

❧

"Who shall stand in His holy place? He that has clean hands, and a pure heart." Psalm 24:3b,4a

❧

Psalm 63:4b; Proverbs 6:10,11a, Lamentations 3:64; Matthew 25:21

Writing

In school, be careful to learn

How to write legibly (good) and neat.

Forming each letter carefully --

To make reading your words a treat.

You should be proud of all you do,

Not settling (being satisfied) with "second best."

Making others struggle (find it hard) to read

What they would consider (think is) a mess!

Good writing is needed to insure (make sure of) success

In almost any profession (job) you will gain.(get).

Make your notes and letters

So to read them is not a strain (hard).

"And whatsoever ye do, do it heartily (your best), as to the Lord, and not unto men." Colossians 3:23
"Whether therefore ye eat, or drink, or whatsoever ye do, do all to the glory of God." I Corinthians 10:31

Proverbs 3:3; Isaiah 8:1a; 30:8;
Jeremiah 30:2; 36:2a; II Corinthians 2:9; Galatians 1:20;
I John 1:4; 2:1; Jude 3; Revelation 1:11,19

Stealing

Stop! You must not take it!

It doesn't belong to you.

No one may see you steal

But God sees all that you do.

If you find you're guilty,

You must try to make things right.

The owner will forgive you

And your heart with God will be right.

Not just by taking someone's things --

You can steal in many ways,

You can spoil someone's reputation
(what one thinks of them)

And guilt is what stealing pays!

❧❧

"You should not steal." Exodus 20:15,
"Ye shall not steal, neither deal falsely, neither lie
to one another." Leviticus 19:11

❧❧

Hosea 4:1,2a; Matthew 19:18; Romans 2:21;
I Thessalonians 4:12a

Smoking

I had an uncle who smoked a lot --
Many cigarettes each day!
He got started through his older brother
Who did not know he was leading him astray.

My uncle died from "Emphysema"
And my dad felt really bad,
So he decided that he had better quit --
And the very next day he had!

There are posters that warn of danger --
Pictures of lungs black as coal!
You are constantly poisoning your body
Not keeping it healthy and whole.

Once you start it is very hard to quit!
A captive of Satan you've become.
Those who smoke think they look really "smart"
But, in reality are really dumb!

There are many, many ways to have fun
To feel good and do things with friends --
Be careful not to harm your body
Or your friends to bad habits you may send!

❧❧

"Know ye not that ye are the temple (house) of God,
and that the Spirit of God dwells in you?"
I Corinthians 3:16; "I will take heed to my ways,
that I sin not..." Psalm 39:1a

❧❧

Psalm 51:10; Romans 6:6;12:1; I Corinthians 6:19,20

Drinking

Just a little drink can't hurt, can it?
But you can never just stop with one!
To please others, you may choose to continue
Until you can't undo what you've done.

You develop a "taste" for the bitter stuff
And now it is too hard to quit.
Besides, your friends keep on encouraging you
And into "your crowd" you want to fit!

Alcohol numbs (paralyzes) a person's mind,
Causes them to do what they "would not."
It's costly and a smelly habit --
With Satan's lies you have been bought!

Liquor changes one's personality,
Causes some to become very cruel --
Accidents and death may even result
So "stay away from the stuff" is the rule!

Your ability to think right is gone,
You may think killing yourself is "hip" --
The best way to avoid all this trouble
Is to refrain (keep from) taking that first sip!

❧❧

"My son, if sinners entice thee, consent thou not."
Proverbs 1:10; "Enter not into the path of the
wicked, and go not in the way of evil men."
Proverbs 4:14

❧❧

Proverbs 14:12; 20:1, Isaiah 28:7a

Gambling

To gamble is to take great chance --
Just hoping that you will win!
But to throw away what you have earned
Is, in God's sight, a great sin.

If you're trusting God with your life --
Every need He will supply!
But if, through greed you want much more,
You may choose with great odds (chance) to try.

To win much money with uncertain (iffy) bets
On horses or gambling wheels --
You will find much to your regret (sorrow)
That Satan your wealth gladly steals!

You must trust the Lord
Your every need to provide (give to you)
And not yield (say yes) to temptation --
But in His will to abide! (live)

❧

"For what is a man profited, if he shall gain the whole
world, and lose himself?" Matthew 16:26a

❧

Ecclesiastes 3:6a; Luke 9:25;
Philippians 3:7

***See "Racetrack"

Feet

Wonder what you'd do without feet?
They take you where you want to go!

But if you do not guide (steer) them aright,
They can become a foe (enemy)!

Be careful of the places they take you!
Beware of traps into which you can fall --

Places that do not honor the Lord (He dislikes)...
Places to where Satan will call.

Go to school and go to church
And visit with neighbors and friends.

Deliver a gift to someone who's sick --
You will reap big "dividends!" (reward)

෧෬෩

"I have refrained my feet from every evil way, that I
may keep Thy word." Psalm 119:101; "Thy word is a lamp
unto my feet, and a light unto my path." Psalm 119:105

෧෬෩

Proverbs 4:14,18,26; Ecclesiastes 11:9; Romans 10:15

Heart

Your heart is so amazing!
The many jobs it does for you!
It sends your blood through arteries and veins
And they number quite a few!!
It may beat for a hundred years or more
If you are careful to treat it right --
But most people do not live that long
For sometimes bad things they must fight.
You may hurt it in an accident
Or be sick for quite some time
But God knows just how long it will last.
Live for Him and long life YOU may find!

✿✿✿

But God's Word tells us this:
If our heart is right with God above,
When death comes, we will live again --
Our hearts will know forever His love!

✿✿✿

"Wait on the Lord: be of good courage, and he shall
strengthen your heart: wait, I say, on the Lord." Psalm 27:14;
"The Lord is my strength and my shield, my heart trusted in him,
and I am helped; therefore my heart greatly rejoices and
with my song I will praise Him." Psalm 28:7

✿✿✿

Psalm 9:1; 13:5; 19:8,14; 22:26; 24:3,4; 32:11; 37:4; 51:10,
53:1; 61:2; 62:8; 66:18; 69:32; 73:26; 77:6; 78:8b; 84:2b;
86:11,12; 97:11; 101:2b,5b; 111:1; 112:7,8a; 119:2,10,
11,34, 69b; 141:4a; 147:3
Proverbs 2:2; 3:3,5; 4:23; 12:20,25; 13:12; 14:30.
15:13-15,28; 16:5a; 17:22; 23:7a,12,17,26.
Jeremiah 15:16; 17:9; 29:13; Daniel 1:8

✿✿✿

Matthew 12:34; 15:8,19; Mark 7:21-23; 12:30;
John 14:27; Romans 10:9,10; II Corinthians 9:7;
Ephesians 5:19; 6:6; Colossians 3:22; II Timothy 2:22;
Hebrews 10:22; I Peter 1:22

Love

The Bible tells us to "love one another"
But that's not always easy to do!
People are not always kind to us —
Can't we be mean to them, too?

No! You must "do unto others"
As you would have them do to you!
Will loving treatment "turn the tables"
(make a difference?) "A soft answer turns away
wrath" (anger) -you will find this true!

Real love forgives and forgets
Things that people do that are wrong!
Don't let their actions make you to sin —
With everyone you must try to "get along!"
(be friends)

""For if ye love them which love you, what reward have
ye...? Matthew 5:46; "Thou shalt love thy neighbor as
thyself." Matthew 19:19b; "Love your enemies, do good
to them which hate you, and pray for them which
despitefully use you." Luke 6:27,28; "...love one
another, as I have loved you..." John 13:34

Joshua 22:5; Judges 16:15b; Psalm 97:10a; 119:132

Honesty

To be truthful is a must!
Dishonest you must not be --

You may be able to fool someone
But God will always know and see!

Every word of God is true
And His promises He keeps --

So, if you do not tell the truth,
His disfavor (anger)
you will reap (get)!

Surely you would not like it
If someone "pulled the wool
over your eyes" --

So treat them as you would yourself...
Ask God for His strength to supply (give you
what you need).

❧❧

"...lead a quiet and peaceable life in all godliness
and honesty." I Timothy 2:2b; "...lead me in
thy truth, and teach me..." Psalm 25:5a

❧❧

Joshua 24:14a; I Kings 2:4b; Psalm 43:3a; 51:6; 86:11;
119:30a; Proverbs 8:7; 12:17; 23:23; John 14:6; 17:17;
Ephesians 6:14a; II Corinthians 4:2; III John 4

Thankfulness

How does one express thankfulness?
To show real appreciation?
Letting one know they are a blessing,
Stating heartfelt appreciation?

Just make certain that your "Thank You"
Is not merely a platitude (nice saying).
Is your thought pure and genuine (real) --
An "attitude of gratitude"?

Some can detect words so phony (not right) --
That are not coming from the heart.
You must harbor (have) a true intention (meaning)
And from honesty not depart.

How important is quick response (action)
So that time does not long elapse (pass by)
For thanks should be spontaneous (quick),
Delay from its graciousness (kindness) taps.
(takes away).

"As you would that men should do to you, do ye also to them
likewise. For if ye love them which love you, what thank have ye?
for sinners also love those that love them." Luke 6:31-33
"Give, and it shall be given unto you...For with the same
measure that ye mete withal it shall be measured to
you again." Luke 38

Psalm 50:14a; 107:21; 150:6; Romans 1:21a;
I Corinthians 15:57; II Corinthians 9:15; Ephesians 5:20;
Colossians 2:7; I Thessalonians 5:18

Contentment

How do you act day by day?
Are you usually happy or sad?
Contentment means you accept what happens
Whether it's good or bad!

If you are wanting to follow God's will,
He will do what's best for you!
You need not worry or panic
Whether disappointments are many or few.

Are you satisfied with what you own?
Or think life's not treating you fair?
Put your trust in God, He loves you!
He's promised your burdens to bear!

So relax, accept what God sends your way...
He will always provide what you need.
Accept what He gives -- don't murmur or fret,
Your every request He will heed (answer).

"I have learned, in whatsoever state I am, therewith
to be content." Philippians 4:11-13; "...be content
with such things as ye have: for He hath said,
"I will never leave thee or forsake thee."
Hebrews 11:5 b,c, 6; "...godliness with content is
great gain...follow after righteousness, godliness,
faith, love, patience, meekness..." I Timothy 6:6-11

***See "My Riches"

Happiness

Do you want to be happy, not sad,
In all of the things that you do?

Will others see a pleasant person?
Will they get a smile from you?

Happiness is a result of joy
That God can put in your heart.

You can encourage others
If your day with the Lord you will start.

When you have peace with the Lord
You can be a blessing to others.

May they see each day His love in you --
Give a smile to your sisters and brothers!

❦

"Be glad in the Lord, and rejoice...shout for joy..."
Psalm 32:11;
"Happy is that people, whose God is the Lord."
Psalm 144:15b

❦

Psalm 146:5; Proverbs 3:13;15:13;16:20b,
17:22; John 13:17

Joy!

Everyone wants to be happy!
Never to be discouraged or sad.
But this is not possible all of the time
For life has its good and its bad!

Happiness may come and go --
It depends on times, places and things.
But these are all so uncertain
And often, the opposite they bring.

But God says you can know real JOY!
Even when things go wrong --
For, if you put your life in His hands,
He can fill your heart with song!

He'll always be there to comfort bring
For whatever trouble comes your way --

You'll know that He's in control
And God's joy is in your heart to stay!

"Now the God of hope fill you with all joy and peace
in believing that ye may abound in hope, through the
power of the Holy Spirit." Romans 15:13
"I will rejoice in the Lord, I will joy in the God of my
salvation." Habakkuk 3:18

Proverbs 21:15; Isaiah 55:12a; John 15:11; 16:22c,24,
Romans 5:11; 15:13; Galatians 5:22;
James 1:2; I Peter 1:8

Jealousy

They say it's the "little green monster"
That makes you jealous of someone,
But it's the devil who gets the credit --
It's his work in you begun!

He makes you think evil thoughts --
Perhaps covet (want) what someone owns --
A great guitar like you had wished for,
Maybe the latest I-pod or cell phone.

Perhaps someone was praised instead of you
And you thought "it wasn't fair!" (right)
Don't place your hopes on earthly things
They can just bring you deep despair (sadness).

Always try to think good thoughts --
Don't let Satan get the best of you.
God will supply your every need --
Praise to Him is what is due.

"And the spirit of jealousy came upon him..."
Numbers 5:14a; "Love works no ill to his
neighbor: therefore love is the fulfilling of the law."
Romans 13:10

Psalm 13:4a; 77:2a; 108:12,13a; I Corinthians
12:31a

Selfishness

You must not selfish be --

Wanting to have more than others!

Not ever wanting to share

With your sisters or your brothers.

You may not have as much as they --

This should not make you angry or sad.

Try to be satisfied and never complain

But for their successes be glad.

God knows how much is best for you

So be happy with what you own.

It may be God's will to give you more

But His plan is for you alone!

❧❦☙

"...you should not covet." Romans 7:7c
"...covet earnestly the best gifts." I Corinthians 12:31a

❧❦☙

Exodus 20:17; Colossians 3:5; Hebrews 13:5

Giving

Do you like to give more than take?

Just for yourself are you living?

To satisfy (make yourself feel good) your needs only

And to others you don't enjoy giving?

The most wonderful Gift ever given

Was God's Son, the Father's greatest treasure!

So, we too, must love as He did

And give to bring others pleasure (joy).

We must unselfish be --

Whatever we have to be sharing

For then, only then, will an unbeliever know

That God's love is prompting (helping) our caring!

❧

"Give to him that asks of you, from him that would
borrow of thee turn not thou away." Matthew 5:42;
"Freely ye have received, freely give." Matthew 10:8b

❧

Psalm 30:12b; 75:1; 92:1, 118:1; Jeremiah 13:16a;
Matthew 19:21; Mark 10:21; Luke 6:38; Romans 12:20

God

Do you want to know who God is?

Then you must read the Bible through.

It tells you all about Him

And what He expects of you!

You can see in the world around you

All the wonderful things He's created (made)

and how He cares for each living thing.

Learn the rules for your life that He's stated (said).

To live in Heaven with God some day

You must give your life back to Him.

There you will see Him forever!

Where you'll know His joy to the brim! (top)

ఆశ్రా

'When I consider thy heavens, the work of thy fingers, the moon and the stars, which thou hast ordained... Psalm 8:3,4;
"Thou art the God that doest wonders..." Psalm 77:14;
"Remember now thy Creator in the days of thy youth..."
Ecclesiastes 12:1a

ఆశ్రా

Psalm 78:7,35; 81:1a; 84:11; Isaiah 40:28,29

Bible

Do you know you have a guidebook
That was written just for you?
On every subject you could want
It has some rules for you!

It tells you how to live right,
How to know success --
How to please your God above
And see Him guide and bless.

How to conquer Satan and evil,
To spread His love to all.
To know His will for your life --
He delights when on Him you call.

Try to read it every day.
Apply its instructions always.
Memorize and share it with others.
Know God and give Him praise.

"I will delight myself in thy statues: I will not forget
thy word." Psalm 119:16; "Every word of God is pure:
he is a shield unto them that put their trust in Him."
Proverbs 30:5

Psalm 119:16, 42; Romans 10:17;
II Corinthians 6:7; I Thessalonians 2:13;
Philippians 2:16; Colossians 3:16;
I Thessalonians 2:13; Hebrews 4:12

Truth

Can you trust the Bible?
It's claim that it is really true?

You will find, as you do read it
That its truths will speak to you.

No-one has ever proved it wrong --
It has answers for every need.

You must decide if it is God's Word
And let it speak to you.

Haters of God try to prove it false
But they have never yet succeeded!

You can have eternal life
If God's rules for your life are heeded.

"O how I love thy law! It is my meditation all the day."
Psalm 119:97: "Thy word is a lamp unto my feet,
and a light unto my path." Psalm 119:105;
"Thy law is truth..." Psalm 119:142b

Psalm 119:11, 97, 130, 165

Faith

Faith is believing
In something you cannot see!
To accept the advice or teaching
That "for your best" would be.

To prove that you have "faith" in a chair,
You must sit on it to prove its worth.
For faith in God, you must believe His Word --
That He alone can give you "new birth."

With faith, you must believe
That God exists and created everything.
That, as a sinner, you cannot be acceptable to God
And no payment for your sins can you bring.

You must believe Jesus, God's Son, died for you
And ask Him to forgive all your sin.
Then put your life under His control --
Then, to Heaven, you will enter in!

❧❧

"...the just shall live by faith." Romans 1:17;
"So then faith cometh by hearing and hearing by
the word of God." Romans 10:17

❧❧

Matthew 17:20,21; Luke 7:50; Romans 1:8.
II Corinthians 5:7; Galatians 2:20; 3:26;
Ephesians 2:8,9; 3:17; I Timothy 6:12;
Hebrews 11:6

Works

Do you think you can go to Heaven
By trying to please God by works...

For there is nothing that you can do
To gain "brownie points" or perks...

We are born to sin against God
And the only way we can be saved

Is to admit to God that we have sinned
And accept the Gift that He gave...

His only Son, who died for us,
To Heaven is the only way...

Don't put off this important choice --
You should make this decision today!

"Not by works of righteousness which we have done,
but according to his mercy he saved us..." Titus 3:5,8
"(God) renders to every man according to his
work." Psalms 62:12; "Not of works, lest any man
should boast." Ephesians 2:9; "If by grace,
then it is no more of works; otherwise, grace is
no more grace." Romans 11:6a

Matthew 5:16; 23:5a; Hebrews 10:24

Trust

Faith means putting your "trust" in something --
Have you ever sat in a chair?
You said you "thought" it would hold you up?
But you didn't know 'til you put yourself there!

To say that you believe in God
And that He died to take away your sin...
To have such faith you must place your trust in Him
And let His holy spirit live within.

You must put your life in His strong hands
And let Him guide your thoughts...
Obeying His Word in your daily life --
Doing only the things that you ought.

❧

"...Put your trust in the Lord." Psalm 4:5; "Let all those that
put their trust in thee rejoice..." Psalm 5:11; "O Lord,
in thee do I put my trust." Psalm 7:1; "Faith is the substance
of things hoped for, the evidence of things not seen..."
Hebrews 11:1; "And they that know thy name will put
their trust in thee: for thou, Lord, hast not forsaken them
that seek thee." Psalm 9:10

❧

Psalm 16:1; 18:2; 20:7; 31:1; 34:8, 22; 36:7; 62:8a;
71:1,3; 73:28; 91:4; 118:8,9 ; Proverbs 3:5; 29:25;
Matthew 11:28,29; I Timothy 4:10

Believing

Faith is not dependent on sight --
It is trust in the Word of the Lord.
Trusting the One Who has promised
To never go back on His Word!
God is the anchor we hold to --
One Who is trustworthy and sure!
Through every trouble and trial,
You know His power will endure (last).

You must be careful not to trust in self
Or put trust in any man --
No matter how strong they seem to be,
To outdo God they never can.
So put your hand in His strong grasp (hold).
Count on his power for you --
With faith as small as a mustard seed,
You will see with awe what He can do!!

☙❧

"...the just shall live by faith." Habakkuk 2:4b; "...put your
trust in the Lord." Psalm 4:5b; "Lord, thou hast heard
the desire of the humble." Psalm 10:17a; "And Jesus
answering...said...have faith in God." Mark 11:22; "For by
grace are ye saved through faith..." Ephesians 2:8a; "...to him
that works not but believes on him...his faith is counted for
righteousness." Romans 4:5; "So then faith cometh by
hearing, and hearing by the word of God." Romans 10:17;
" Now faith is the substance of things hoped for, the
evidence of things not seen." Hebrews 11:1

☙❧

Matthew 9:22b; 29b; 14:31b; 17:20b; 21:21b; Mark 11:22;
Luke 17:5; 18:8b; Acts 26:18; Romans 1:17b; 12:3; 14:23b;
I Corinthians 16:13; II Corinthians 5:7; Galatians 3:11;
Ephesians 3:17; 6:16; Hebrews 6:12; 12:2; James 1:3,6;
I Peter 1:7, II Peter 1:5+; I John 5:4

Salvation

Do you know if you are "saved?"
If you are, do you <u>know</u> just when
You asked God to forgive your sin?
Then you <u>don't</u> have to do it again!

Jesus said when you belong to Him,
He will never let you go --
You are now His precious child.
He will protect you from every foe (enemy).

"As far as the east is from the west" --
(Around the world, they NEVER MEET!!)
God has thrown away your sin --
That's a promise that can't be beat!!

So, don't put off this important decision
For you don't know how long you will live --
To know that you will live forever!
And to you, all God's blessings He will give.

"As far as the east is from the west, so far hath he removed
our transgressions from us." Psalm 103:12; "Neither is there
salvation in any other: for there is no other name under heaven,
given among men, whereby we must be saved." Acts 4:12;
"For I am not ashamed of the gospel of Christ: for it is the
power of God unto salvation to every one that
believeth..." Romans 1:16

Psalm 13:5b; 27:7; 62:2a, 6; 118:21;
Isaiah 12:2; 51:6c; Ephesians 6:17;
I Peter 1:5

God's Ten Commandments

(1) You should have no other gods before me.
(2) You should not make unto thee any graven image
or any likeness of any thing that is in heaven
above...in the earth beneath...in the water
under the earth. You should not bow down thyself
to them, nor serve them...
(3) You should not take the name of the Lord thy God
in vain...
(4) Remember the Sabbath Day, to keep it holy.
Six days you shall labor and do all thy work:
but the seventh day is the Sabbath...in it you
shall not do any wok...
(5) Honor thy father and thy mother...
(6) You shall not kill.
(7) You shall not commit adultery.
(8) You shall not steal.
(9) You shall not bear false witness against
thy neighbor.
(10) You shall not covet...anything that is thy
neighbor's.

(Exodus 20:3,4,5a; 7-9; 12-17)

Church

Do you think church is boring?

Do you just color pictures or read?

Not listening to the sermon?

God's Word to obey or heed?

You may not understand everything

But attention try to pay...

For your Heavenly Father --

To you has something to say!

The church is a wonderful place

To encourage a stranger or friend,

Speak a kind word or offer to help

And misunderstandings mend.

"I was glad when they said unto me, Let us go
into the house of the Lord." Psalm 122:1
"Speaking...in psalms and hymns and spiritual
songs, singing and making melody in your heart
to the Lord." Ephesians 5:19

John 4:23b,24; 9:31b; Hebrews 10:25,
I John 1:3b,7

***See "All of Life"
"Be Involved"
"My Riches"

Worship

Worship requires one's full attention --

Your mind and heart greatly stirred,

Constantly giving God the glory

As you sing, pray and hear God's Word.

Letting the Lord speak to your heart

And applying His Word to your life.

Thanking him for blessings given

Asking forgiveness for selfish strife.

A prayer for forgiveness, if needed,

And strength for a witness to be --

Then going forth in God's strength alone,

His control of your life to see.

"Give unto the Lord the glory due unto his name:
bring an offering...worship the Lord in the beauty
of holiness." I Chronicles 16:29;
"O come let us worship and bow down: let us
kneel before the Lord our maker." Psalm 95:6

Psalm 29:2; 66:4; John 4:23,24; Ephesians 5:19;

*** See "ALL OF LIFE"

Unity

Unity means "to be as one " --
To work together when you disagree.
Not to insist on your own way,
For then God's blessing you'll see.

To argue is NOT the best way
Or to claim that you alone are right!
For if you all strive to see God's will,
It will avoid a nasty fight.

Prayer is the way to solve problems,
To seek God's will in everything --
Instead of confusion and grieving,
The answer to problems 'twill bring.

God does not desire confusion,
He desires His will to be done --
For never is there disagreement
Between the Father and His Son!

❧

"Lord, my heart is not haughty..." Psalm 131:a; "Behold, how good and how pleasant it is for brethren to dwell together in unity." Psalm 133:1; "...when I became a man, I put away childish things..." I Corinthians 13:11b; "Endeavoring to keep the unity of the Spirit in the bond of peace." Ephesians 4:3

❧

Romans 12:16; 15:6; I Corinthians 1:10; Philippians 1:27a; 2:2,3; 4:2; Colossians 3:12,13; II Timothy 1:7; I Peter 3:8,9

Allowance

Do you get an allowance?
Earn money by doing chores?
Do you spend it all or save it?
Into a "piggybank" it pours?

Do you know who helped you
To do what you had to do?
It was your Heavenly Father --
Should He not be "paid" something, too?

The Bible says that we should give
A tenth of all we earn.
A dime out of every dollar
Is the lesson you should learn.

If you honor God in this way,
He will bless you in all your tasks.
For God always gives us more
Than we could ever ask!

"Honor the Lord with your substance, and with the
first fruits of all your increase; so shall thy
(barns) be filled with plenty..." Proverbs 1:9,10
"The blessing of the Lord, it makes rich, and He
adds no sorrow with it." Proverbs 10:22

Psalm 112:1-3a; Matthew 6:19-21; II Corinthians 9:7

***See "My Riches"

Tithing

Did you know your dad pays "taxes,"
To the U.S. Government each year?
If he fails to fill out income forms,
A severe (bad) penalty he must fear.

The money helps the government to pay
For roads and bridges, firemen and police.
Without these funds, crime might increase (get bigger)
And all necessary building would cease. (stop)

But there's Someone else Who needs to share
At least a tenth of what we earn --
A dime of every dollar we should give --
The rule of "tithing" we must learn.

It is God Who gives us the talent
And strength to do our daily tasks --
We must gladly give from what we earn
And even more than what God asks.

❧❧

"Give unto the Lord the glory due His name:
bring an offering, and come into His courts." Psalm 96:8;
"It is more blessed to give than receive." Acts 20:35b

❧❧

Mark 10:21; Luke 11:41a; 12:33a; Malachi 3:10

***See "My Riches"

Prayer

We all know how to talk with our parents
And spend time on the phone with a friend.

We thank all those who give us nice gifts,
Sometimes, a letter we send.

How can we thank our Heavenly Father?
And spend some time with Him every day?

He wants to talk with us, His children
And He does this, as to Him we pray.

He knows our needs but wants us to share
Our thoughts, our wishes and daily cares.

For He has promised our prayers He will hear.
And a sad heart to lovingly cheer.

"...the prayer of the upright is His delight." Proverbs 15:8b;
"Be careful for nothing; but in everything by prayer
and thanksgiving let your requests be made known
unto God." Philippians 4:6

Psalm 65:2; I Thessalonians 5:17; James 5:16

***See "A Toddler's Prayer
"Don't Let Go"
"My Prayer"
"Praying"
"The 5-Finger Prayer"

Witnessing

When finding something "really good!"

You want to share it with others...

To tell them how they can find it too

Becomes really important to you.

You found the best thing in all the world

When you asked to become God's child.

So don't be afraid to tell your friends

How they, too, can be reconciled (made right with God),

It's the best thing you can do for them...

Then they'll join you in Heaven some day!

God will bless you if you share

How they, too, can follow God's way.

❧❧

"That I may publish with the voice of thanksgiving,
and tell of all thy wondrous works." Psalm 26:7
"The fruit of the righteous is a tree of life; and
he that wins souls is wise." Proverbs 11:30

❧❧

Matthew 5:13-16; 28:19a; Mark 16:15

Gifts

Do you know what you can do best?

Then try to develop those gifts.

God will give you opportunities galore

Others' burdens and spirit to lift.

You will be happy and others will, too,

As you seek to use your gifts each day.

God has promised to bless your good deeds

As you read His word daily and pray.

You must always remember this:

That your talent is from God above

So do not boast of your gifts

But use them with humility and love.

"Neglect not the gift that is in thee..." I Timothy 4:14a;
"Every good and every perfect gift is from above
and comes down from the Father..." James 1:17

Romans 12:6+; I Corinthians 12:31a;
II Timothy 1:6a; I Peter 4:10

***See "Serving"
"Big or Little"
"Success""

Talents

Do you know what a "talent" is?
It's something you can do quite well.
And if you try your very best,
Some day you may even excel!

Can you play an instrument or sing?
Can you kick or throw a ball?
Can you draw a picture, write a poem,
Or even a car overhaul?

You can use your gift to bring joy to others,
As a doctor, save many lives!
Be careful not to waste any gift God's given you --
For His will a wise boy and girl strives.

You will be happy and others will, too,
As you seek to use your gifts each day.
God has promised to bless your good deeds
As you read His word daily and pray.

❧❧

"Covet earnestly the best gifts..." I Corinthians 12:31a
"Neglect not the gift that is in thee..." I Timothy 4:14a

❧❧

Psalm 33:2,3; Matthew 25:21; Romans 12:6-8

Coveting

You don't have to be old to "covet" --
That means "to want more and more things."

You might see something all your friends have
And a dissatisfied (not wanted) feeling it brings.

You'd like to have that item (thing) too
And not having it brings you pain --

Now, not satisfied with what you own,
You work 'til that object (thing) you gain (get).

It may not be something you really need.
God has said "all your needs He'll supply (give you)!"

So try to be satisfied with what you own,
Such wisdom (good thinking) you'll not be able to buy!

God wants you to "covet" (really want) His good gifts
And He'll give you all that you need --

You'll always be happy when in His will
And not be a victim of greed (more than you need).

"...for your Father knows what things ye have need of,
before ye ask Him." Matthew 6:8b
"God shall supply all your need, according to His
riches in glory by Christ Jesus." Philippians 4:19

Acts 20:24a, Romans 7:7e; I Corinthians 12:31a

Body

Your body is a temple!

And your spirit lives within...

And who will rule your spirit?

Whoever you let in!

Let God dwell (live) within you

And let Him guide your soul

For He is the One Who made you --

To please Him should be your goal.

Your eyes, your ears, your hands, your feet...

All should be turned over to Him.

Satan will try to trip you up

But then you'll have power over him!

"Let not sin reign in your mortal body, that ye should obey
it in the lusts thereof...neither yield your members as
instruments of unrighteousness unto sin: but yield yourself
unto God...to whom you yield yourself servant to obey, his
servant you are to whom you obey..." Romans 6:12;13a; 16a

Psalm 139:14-16; Luke 11:34; Romans 8:10,13;
I Corinthians 6:18-20

***See "My Car"

Exercise

Your body needs exercise to properly grow
Or you will end up "fat" or weak.
You might do sit-ups or lift weights
Until you reach a desired peak.

But don't forget to walk each day
At least a mile or two --
You will see how much stronger you'll feel
And it will help you when feeling blue.

You must exercise your body
But also your mind and heart.
Don't put things off until you are old -
While you're still young, you should start.

"...your body is the temple of the Holy Ghost...therefore,
glorify God in your body..." I Corinthians 6:19,20
"Exercise thyself...unto godliness." I Timothy 4:7

Acts 24:16; I Timothy 4:8; III John 2

Sleep

Is it important to get plenty of rest?
If a healthy, strong body you want to build,
You must give it time to recuperate
(get better)
And sleeping is when this is fulfilled (done).

You need to slow down after work and play,
Your body cannot keep going and going!
Like a robot, if you never take time to stop,
You may see your healthy body stop growing!

Even strong athletes know how imporant this is
So obey your mom and dad...
When they say "it's off to bed for you!"
Be obedient -- don't make them grumpy or sad!

❧

"...they shall rest in their beds." Isaiah 57:2b;
"...God rested from all the work which He created and
made." Genesis 2:2b

❧

Exodus 16:30; 31:17b; Psalm 23:3; 92:2b;
Proverbs 30:17

Play

Playing, jumping, running and walking
Is far better than sitting and talking!
Make your body breathe hard and sweat.
Every day good exercise get!

Your body needs fresh air to grow,
And your muscles need a workout --
And so do your heart and lungs,
Of this there is no doubt!

So ride your bicycle and run,
Do some tumbling or roller-skate,
Join a sports team in the summer --
Don't hesitate (think twice) to participate.

You'll have fun and new friends, too
If you don't sit at home and mope!
Exercise polishes your skills
And teaches you how to cope.

❧❧

"Why do we sit still?" Jeremiah 8:14a
"Exercise thyself unto godliness." I Timothy 4:7b

❧❧

Acts 24:16; I Timothy 4:8

Sports

Do you like to be outdoors?

Do you like to really compete?

Then a sport may be just the thing

If your fears you can defeat.

Practice helps your skills to grow,

And to excel you must really try.

But if you cannot make the grade,

Don't be a baby and cry.

Do not try to be the "star" --

A team player you must be.

Always do your very best

And the victory you will see.

༺❦༻

"Let nothing be done through strife or vainglory:
but in lowliness of mind, let each esteem other better
than themselves." Philippians 2:3;
"I seek not my own glory..." John 8:50a

༺❦༻

Romans 12:1; I Corinthians 1:31b, 4:7,
6:19,20, 9:27a, 10:31; I Timothy 4:8,12,14a

Competition

A contest is always fun.
Makes you want to try very hard
To do your very best.

And its great to be the winner --
To receive the prize that's given!
But think of all the rest...
Who for the prize had striven.

Every one who ran in the race
Was also trying to win,
And are disappointed to be left behind.
So don't try to "rub it in."

Be a gracious winner...or a loser, too,
And never give up trying!
There's usually another time or place
When you won't end up crying!!

"Know ye not that they which run in a race run all, but one
receives the prize? So run that ye may obtain."
I Corinthians 9:24-26

Proverbs 4:11,12; Ecclesiastes 9:11;
Philippians 2:16; Hebrews 12:1,2

Judging

Many things the word "judging" may mean:
A rating, an opinion, decision or penalty.
In all of your lifetime you may find
Any number of these you will probably see.

In athletic competition, after you have performed,
There will be those who judge just how you did --
They look for certain requirements (rules) and bonus points,
How you "score" on an established grid (chart).

Other people form an "opinion" of you
Based on your appearance, talk or deeds --
How you dress, your habits, what you say --
You must be careful when sowing (planting) these seeds.

A "penalty" is rendered (given) for something done wrong,
However (even if) trivial (not important) or serious it
may be,
I'm sure you'll not murder but we all do tell lies,
So truthfulness let everyone see!

You'll find that many times in your life,
Decisions you'll be asked to make --
Be careful to consider the outcome for all
To the Lord all your options (choices) take.

❧❧

"God judges the righteous..." Psalms 7:11;
"Judge not, that ye be not judged." Matthew 7:1;
Luke 6:37a; Know ye not that they which run in a race
run all, but one receives the prize? So run, that ye may
obtain." I Corinthians 9:24; "...the trial of your faith being much
more precious than of gold that perishes..." I Peter 1:7a

❧❧

Psalm 51:4; Jeremiah 11:20a; Romans 2:1,2; John 5:22;
Hebrews 12:1; James 4:12b

Popularity

People may really like you
And you may not lack for friends.

That's when you must be careful
Of the "signals" (signs) that you send --

Don't only brag about yourself
And the things that you can do --

Don't make your conversations
Center only and all around you!

For soon your friends will leave you,
Seeing how selfish you are --

If you want to keep your friends,
Don't make yourself the "star."

They will like you more and more
If important you make them feel --

Don't let fame "go to your head,"
Show them your friendship is real!

"For thou, Lord, wilt bless the righteous; with favor
wilt thou compass him as with a shield." Psalm 5:12
"So shall you find favor and good understanding
in the sight of God and man." Proverbs 3:4

Proverbs 8:35; 11:27; 12:2; 22:21; 31:30a

Heroes

There are people you will like

And try to imitate.

They could be masters of their sport

And excellent scores do rate.

They may be popular and well known,

And like them you'd like to be.

But be careful whom you pick --

From bad examples flee!

Always try to be your best

For some day you may become,

By living as God wants you to,

A hero to daughter or son.

"Look unto Jesus, the author and finisher of our faith,
who for the joy that was set before Him
endured the cross..." Hebrews 12:2

Psalm 49:16,17; 52:7; Hebrews 11, 12:1:2

Humility

It is good to like yourself!

To be glad of what you can do.

But you must not become proud and think

That others are not as good as you!

For all that you excel in

Is a gift from God above!

So you must give thanks to Him

And treat everyone else with love.

Use the gifts God has given you

To be the best you can be.

If you ask for His help every day,

His constant help you will see.

❧

"And whosoever shall exalt himself shall be abased;
and he that shall humble himself shall be exalted." Matthew 23:12
"...be clothed with humility: for God resists the proud,
and gives grace to the humble." I Peter 5:5b,c

❧

Proverbs 15:33; 22:4; James 4:6b

Minds

Your mind stores up everything
That you have come to know...

All you want to remember
As the years all come and go.

You'll remember places
And facts and figures (numbers), too,
How to solve your problems
And plan what you must do.

Try to store what's good and best
And shut out all that's bad --
For what you put inside your head
Can make you sad or glad.

The power to think is wonderful,
A gift from God to you --
But you'll be held responsible
For all you think to do.

❧❧

"Thou wilt keep him in perfect peace, whose mind
is stayed on thee: because he trusts in thee." Isaiah 26:3
"For God hath not given us the spirit of fear, but of power,
and of love, and of a sound mind." II Timothy 1:7

❧❧

I Chronicles 28:9; Nehemiah 4:6c; Proverbs 29:11;
Mark 12:30; Luke 10:27; Acts 17:11; 20:19;
Romans 1:28; 7:23,25; 8:5; 12:2,16; I Cor.1:10; 13:11;
Ephesians 4:17,23,24; Philippians 1:27; 2:3,5;
Colossians 1:21; Titus 1:15; I Peter 1:13; 3:8

Knowledge

There are those who have much knowledge
But their thoughts lead men astray (the wrong way).
They do not know our God
Or want to go His way.

So even if you know a lot,
It doesn't mean you're smart!
To really know God's Word
Is where you ought to start.

For then you will have wisdom
And others you can teach
So they will know God's blessing
And others, too, can reach.

True knowledge comes from God alone
For He created all things --
He will lead and He will guide --
TRUE knowledge He will bring!

"Whoso loves instruction loves knowledge." Proverbs 12:1;
"Who is a wise man and endued with knowledge
among you? Let him show out of a good conversation
his works with meekness of wisdom." James 3:13;
"That ye might be filled with the knowledge of His will
in all wisdom and spiritual understanding."
Colossians 1:9

Exodus 35:31; II Chronicles 1:10a,12a; Proverbs
2:10,11; 12:1; 15:2; 18:15; 20:15; 21:11b; 24:5;
Philippians 1:9; Colossians 1:9,10; 2:3;
James 3:13; II Peter 1:5

***See "Do We Think We Know It All?"

Wisdom

Wisdom is something you cannot buy.
You must learn as you live and grow.
To make good decisions and choices --
It's how you apply what you know.

Wisdom keeps you from foolish (stupid) errors.
So many friends you will probably know --
As they honor your good judgment (decisions),
For advice to you they will go.

The best place to gain such wisdom
Is from God's Word every day --
It will guide your thoughts and actions
As you yield to God and pray.

Who has more wisdom than God above?
Like Him, you should strive to be.
Your life will then be blessed by Him
And His daily guidance (leading) you will see.

❧❧

"...a good understanding have all they that do (God's)
commandments..." Psalm 111:10b; "For wisdom is better
than rubies..." Proverbs 8:11a; "How much better it is
to get wisdom than gold...(and) silver." Proverbs 16:16;
"In whom are hid all the treasures of wisdom and
knowledge." Colossians 2:3; "If any of you lack
wisdom, let him ask of God." James 1:5,6

❧❧

Proverbs 1:1-4,7; 2:1-11; 3:13; 9:10; 15:33; 19:8;
23:4b,23; Ecclesiastes 9:18a; Daniel 2:23a;
Colossians 2:3; James 1:5,6

Thoughts

No-one else knows what you're thinking

Except for the One Who made you!

Be careful what you store in your mind --

Your thoughts control what you do!

You must not desire what others have

Or think on things that are wrong...

For soon you will be out of God's will

And lose your joy and your song.

The worldly person thinks only of self

And crowds God out of his mind.

As one of God's own, you should think

Of things that are good and kind.

❧

"whatsoever things are true...honest...just...pure...
lovely...of good report...think on these things."
Philippians 4:8, "I thought on my ways, and
turned my feet unto thy testimonies." Psalm 119:59

❧

Genesis 6:5; Job 21:27; Psalm 119:11; 139:17,18;
Proverbs 15:26

Choices

Sometimes you will wonder
What it is you should do --

You have to make a choice
And options (choices) are quite a few.

You must not listen to silly advice
Or schemes (plans) that put you in danger,

It's best to listen to those who are wise
Like parents or teachers -- not strangers.

But who do you think is wisest of all?
It's God in Heaven above!

You must decide to follow His will
For He'll always answer with love.

"The steps of a good man are ordered by the Lord:
and he delights in his way." Psalm 37:23,24
"Oh send out thy light and thy truth, let them
lead me." Psalm 43:3

Psalm 25:5; 37:24; Proverbs 3:5-7; 4:11; 16:3;
Ecclesiastes 2:26; Daniel 2:21

Priorities

A priority is putting something first --
Doing all you can to make it come true.
No matter what obstacles you find in your path,
Keep trying is what you must do!

A priority is what you think most important --
You make it your "number one" goal!"
As a Christian, your greatest priority
Is to guard your eternal soul.

You will never lose your salvation
But your testimony you must live.
Don't settle for anything less --
With God's help, your best you must give!

❧❧

"But seek ye first the kingdom of God..." Matthew 6:33;
"...(they) first gave their own souls to the Lord."
II Corinthians 8:5,12; "...many that are first
shall be last: and the last first." Mark 10:31;
12:28-31

❧❧

I John 4:19

Studying

You want to learn as much as you can

For your future to daily prepare.

So read and study material assigned --

To "flake off" you do not dare!

For nothing is more important

As some day you will learn...

All the knowledge you can gain

Will help a good life to earn.

But, most of all, you should absorb (take in)

As much of God's Word as you can...

For He will teach and guide you

To follow His unsurpassed (best) plan!

༺❧༻

"Receive My instruction, and not silver,
and knowledge rather than choice gold." Proverbs 8:10

༺❧༻

Proverbs 10:4b; 21:5a; Ecclesiastes 12:12a;
II Timothy 2:15

Memorizing

Did you know that what you memorize

Will stay forever in your heart?

So be sure to get out your Bible --

To learn God's Word, you'll be smart!

For then God's promises will always be there

To remember. They'll help you each day --

To encourage, guide and strengthen you

And help you to know how to pray.

No one can ever make you forget

And, when in trouble, take away.

The words of God Himself, meant for you --

They'll help you from Him not to stray.

❧❧

"Thy word have I hid in my heart, that I might not sin
against Thee." Psalm 119:11, "I will never forget
Thy precepts..." Psalm 119:93a
Psalm 119:16,33,73b,103,130; John 14:26;
16:4a, II Timothy 3:14,15

Computers

Travel the internet to hundreds of places,
Even study to earn a degree!

Not bound by time or space --
Hours you can spend profitably! (for good)

Instead of one teacher, you'll have many
And all over the world you can go!

You can investigate (learn) any subject
And pick out what you'd like to know.

You can travel to any country.
Meet people from far and near --

You may not have to take any exams (tests)
Or a teacher's grades have to fear!

"When wisdom enters into your heart, and knowledge is
pleasant unto your soul; discretion shall preserve you,
understanding shall keep you." Proverbs 2:10,11
"Wise men lay up knowledge..." Proverbs 10:14

Proverbs 12:1a; 15:2; 18:15; Colossians 1:9; 2:3

Worry

Are you timid -- afraid to try new things?

Worried that you may not succeed (do good)--

And if you fail, people might laugh?

From such fear, you'd like to be freed?

Are you afraid of flying?

Or climbing to a mountaintop?

Or competing in a contest or race?

Don't know how these fears to stop?

God has promised to be with you,

To give you courage and strength --

You must trust Him to help you perform (do well).

You can know quiet through every storm!

❧
"Be strong and of a good courage; be not afraid,
neither be dismayed: for the Lord thy God
is with thee wherever you go." Joshua 1:9
"I can do all things through Christ who strengthens
me." Philippians 4:13

❧
Ezra 7:28b; Psalms 121:1-3; 5-8; Isaiah 41:10;
I Corinthians 16:13; Hebrews 13:5c,6

Fears

There are many things in this life to fear
(be afraid of) --
People and events to make you afraid...

But, if you know God, He will protect you
(keep you safe)
If you trust (believe) in the promises He's made.

"Perfect love casts out fear"
God promises in His holy Word...

So love the Lord with all your heart..
He protects even the smallest bird!

You may be in danger but God will be there
And you will know the peace that He gives...

His eye is always upon those
Who obey Him and for His glory lives.

❧❧

"Say to them that are of a fearful heart, be strong,
fear not..." Isaiah 35:4; "...we may boldly say, the
Lord is my helper, and I will not fear what man
shall do unto me." Hebrews 13:6

❧❧

Psalm 27:3a; Matthew 10:29-31; I John 4:18a,b

Goals

It is always good to set some goals --
Things toward which you will strive
(work hard for),
They will keep you from "falling asleep"
And help keep your dreams alive.

Be sure your goals are good ones,
Worth all the effort you make.
Some goals will be easy to reach.
Others, some risks (chances) you must take.

Don't be lazy and give up.
Keep plugging (trying) to the very end.
Always looking to Jesus,
Your wisest, most caring friend!

"Labor not to be rich." Proverbs 23:4; "Do not go
forth hastily to strive..." Proverbs 25:8a; "I press toward
the mark of the high calling of God in Christ Jesus."
Philippians 3:14

Psalm 127:1a; Proverbs 13:11; Ecclesiastes 2:10c,
21a; 3:13; Luke 6:27; II Timothy 2:5

Obstacles

When you are wanting to go somewhere
And an obstacle gets in your way, (big block)
Do you just "give up" trying again?
And "down in the dumps" (sad) do you stay?
No, you must always "try, try again"
To find a way to succeed (win).
You need to have lots of courage (be brave) --
Find voices of wisdom (good sense) to heed (obey).

There is nothing too hard for God --
With your problems to Him you should go.
He can guide your pathway aright --
Show you the way you should go.
Sometimes he'll give you a "yes" or "no".
Sometimes He'll want you to wait!
But never give up until you do your best
Or know your plan was a mistake (wrong).

ॐ

"God is our refuge and strength, a very present help in trouble."
Psalm 46:1; "He shall call upon me, and I will answer him
I will be with him in trouble, I will deliver him, and honor
him." Psalm 91:15; "Let not your heart be troubled, ye
believe in God, believe also in me." John 14:1 "Is anything
too hard for the Lord?" Genesis 18:14a; "The Lord hears
thee in the time of trouble…" Psalm 20:1; "You are my hiding
place; you shall save me from trouble…" Psalm 32:7a; "Thou
therefore endure hardship, as a good soldier of Jesus
Christ." II Timothy 2:3

ॐ

Psalm 9:13; 31:7a; 32:7; 37:39; 41:1; 46:1, 60:11;
77:2a; 81:7a; 86:7; 108:12,13; Proverbs 11:8a;
John 14:1, 27; II Corinthians 1:4

Catastrophies

Sometimes things will happen in life
That you'll not be able to understand...
This is the time that you must believe
God's in control and trust His hand!

Nothing takes God by surprise
And He always knows what is best...
So do not question or discouraged be --
In all His promises you can rest.

It's up to you how you will react
To things that don't go your way.
Others are carefully watching you
To see what you'll do or say.

You can be a testimony clear
Of God's faithfulness to you
And help all those around
To learn to trust Him too.

❧❧

"For in the time of trouble he shall hide me in his
pavilion; in the secret of his tabernacle shall he
hide me..." Psalm 27:5; "The righteous is
delivered out of trouble." Proverbs 11:8a

❧❧

Psalm 37:23,24; 116:8; 139:2-6

Failure

Would it be a big surprise to you
That sometimes you will fail?

Life will not always be easy --
O'er all your problems to sail!

Even after trying your best,
All may not go as you had planned.

Don't give up and be in despair (sad),
Let new thoughts in your mind take command.

"If at first you don't succeed,
Try, try again" is wise advice --

Take to the Lord your problem,
To worry and fret is not wise.

❧❧

"...there hath not failed one word of all his good
promise …" I Kings 8:56b; "Our soul waits for the Lord:
he is our help and our shield..." Psalm 33:20
"...we glory in tribulations (troubles), knowing
that tribulation works patience." Romans 5:3

❧❧

Psalm 32:8; 48:14; 73:24a; 26, 143:7a

Sorrow

Sometimes there will enter your life --

Things that you cannot control.

Which will bring to you great sorrow --

That, it seems, nothing can console.
(make you feel better)

A death in your family,
An illness that can't be cured --
An accident quite unforeseen,
Harsh (mean) words you've had to endure (take).

When sorrow comes to engulf you,
(make you sad)
On yourself you must not depend --
Turn to God for He sees ALL --
His comfort and peace He will send!

"Weeping may endure for a night, but joy cometh in
the morning." Psalm 30:5; "Hear me speedily, O
Lord; my spirit fails: hide not thy face from me."
Psalm 143:7a; "...concerning them that are asleep,
that ye sorrow not, even as those who have no hope..."
I Thessalonians 4:13,14

John 16:20b, II Corinthians 7:10a; Revelation 21:4

Illness

It seems everyone suffers a cold
Or a headache once in awhile.

Many suffer an illness
But yours lasts more than just a while!

Your days may stretch out "unending!"
With pain your "unwanted guest,"

And you long for relief and comfort --
For days filled once again with zest! (fun)

The Lord knows your situation
And for your life has a plan.

He will work in you His blessed will,
Giving strength, as only HE can!!

"Lord, be merciful unto me: heal my soul...
Psalm 41:4a; "Heal me, O Lord, and I shall be
healed...for thou art my praise." Jeremiah 17:1a;
"And the power of the Lord was present to
heal them." Luke 5:17b

Suffering

There are many ways to suffer...
To know "loss of peace of mind" --
Rejection by a very close friend,
A criticism, harsh and unkind!

The illness of a family member,
Sudden death of parent or friend...
You may feel you've been abandoned,
That "bad luck" days will never end.

You must not give up in despair
But give your burdens to the Lord...
He KNOWS, and CARES, and WORKS
To fulfill promises in His Word.

"Look upon mine affliction and my pain; and forgive all my
sins." Psalm 25:18; "My heart is sore pained within me."
Psalm 55:4a; "Cast thy burden upon the Lord, and He shall
sustain thee." Psalm 55:22; "And they departed...rejoicing that
they were counted worthy to suffer,,,for his name." Acts 5:41;
"There hath no temptation taken you but such as is common
to man: but God is faithful, who will not suffer you to be
tempted above that ye are able; but will with the temptation
make a way to escape, that ye may be able to bear it."
I Corinthians 10:13, "And God shall wipe away all tears from their
eyes; and there shall be no more death, neither sorrow, nor crying,
neither shall there be any more pain; for the former things are
passed away." Revelation 21:4

Psalm 121:3b; I Corinthians 12:26a; Philippians 1:29;
II Timothy 2:12a; I Peter 2:20b; 3:14a,17; 4:16

Hope

Sometimes you'll be discouraged (sad)
And happy again wish to be.
When things begin to change for the better,
Then "hope" you will again see.

Hope gives you brand new chances
When you can begin anew (again),
It gives you time and energy (strength)
To do what you want to do.

To see things happen for the good,
No disappointment to know,
The One Who can give you your greatest hope
Is God, IF to Him you will go.

The greatest hope He can give you
Is a wonderful future with Him --
When that hope becomes a reality (sure),
It's something that can never be dimmed (taken away).

❧

"And now, Lord, what wait I for? My hope is in thee."
Psalm 39:7; "For thou art my hope, O Lord God; thou art
my trust from my youth." Psalm 71:5; "For whatsoever
things were written aforetime were written for our learning,
that we through patience and comfort of the scriptures might
have hope." Romans 15:4,13

❧

Psalm 119:114; 146:5; Romans 8:24, 12:12a;
15:4,13; I Corinthians 15:19; Ephesians 2:12;
Colossians 1:27; I Thessalonians 2:19;
I Timothy 1:1; Titus 1:2; 2:13; 3:7; Hebrews 6:19;
I Peter 1:21; 3:15

Protection

Who can you count on to protect you?
A big brother or your dad?
Maybe, if you're in a fist fight --
But if someone just makes you mad?

There are all kinds of dangers
In a world so full of sin --
There's smoking, drinking, gambling --
And the list will not be thin!

You may desire things you should not,
Your thoughts may go astray (wrong) --
So many things that can trip you up!
Who'll protect you in every way?

God promises to be by your side.
He'll defeat each and every foe.
You need His strength and presence near.
Don't forget, His great power you can know!

"Our soul waits for the Lord; He is our help and our
shield." Psalm 33:20; "God is our refuge and strength,
a very present help in trouble." Psalm 46:1

Psalm 22:19; 23:4; 37:40; 46:1; 108:13; 121:2;
124:8; Hebrews 13:6; Jude 24

***See "D.A.R.E." (Drugs)
"Drinking"
"Smoking"

Guidance

Who should you look to for guidance?
Who will never, ever lead you astray?
Your parents and friends may be of help
But it is to the Lord you should pray!

If you follow in Christ's footsteps
He will lead you to know the truth
And you will never have to question
How you should live your youth.

His Word, the Bible, should be your road map,
If you read it every day
You will find all the help you will need
For in it He shows you His way.

"For thou art my rock and my fortress; therefore for
thy name's sake lead me, and guide me." Psalm 31:3;
"I will instruct thee and teach thee in the way which
thou shalt go; I will guide thee with mine eye."
Psalm 32:8

Psalm 73:24; Proverbs 23:19, Luke 1:79;
John 16:13a; Colossians 2:6

Future

Some day you will have to decide:

*WHAT YOU WOULD LIKE TO BE
*WHAT JOB YOU WILL TAKE
*WHAT MATE YOU WILL CHOOSE
*AND WHERE YOU WILL LIVE...

So be thinking right now
So that when each time comes,
You will know what you want to achieve.

God will bless each choice that you make
If His will for your life you'll believe.

You may get wise advice from parents or friends
But be careful God's Word to heed!

He has a wonderful plan for your life --
And He promises each day to lead.

"You will show me the path of life; in thy presence is
fullness of joy; at Your right hand there are pleasures
forevermore." Psalm 16:11; "The steps of a good man
are ordered by the Lord; and he delights in His way."
Psalm 37:23

Psalm 91:114-16; Proverbs 2:20; 3:1,2; 8:35; 12:4

Dating

When you are in high school,
You'll probably start to date.
You'll find someone that you really like
And a friendship you'll create.

A boy or girl that likes you, too --
It's easy to talk to him or her.
Who likes to do the things you do
And soon special feelings will stir.

But you aren't ready to stick to one beau
For you've many years of schooling ahead.
So try to "date" more than one good friend
And have good times with many instead.

This will help you when it comes time to choose
The one you should some day marry.
To know what you really want in a mate --
And marriage then won't be so scary!

❧❧

"A man that hath friends must show himself friendly."
Proverbs 18:24a; "Even a (youth) is known by his
doings, whether his work be pure, and whether it
be right." Proverbs 20:11; "Unto the pure
all things are pure..." Titus 1:15

Courting

Some day you will want to marry.
What should you like your mate to be?
Slim or fat, happy or grumpy?
Like someone on your "family tree"?

You must be thinking about desirable traits,
Someone who likes the things you do!
You must not settle for something less
Or he (she'll) bring unhappiness to you.

Dating is the time in your youth
That you must determine what you like best,
Not committing yourself to any boy or girl
Until ready your entire life to invest!

So go out with many and not just a few.
Have a good time but do not choose
Until you've had time to know what you want --
Or your youthful, carefree days you will lose.

As a Christian, you will want God's will
In picking your future mate
So seek His will as you consider your future
And carefully select each date.

❧❧

"...Present your bodies a living sacrifice, holy,
acceptable unto God...and be not conformed to this
world: but be transformed by the renewing of your mind,
that you may prove what is that good, and acceptable,
and perfect, will of God." Romans 12:1,2

❧❧

Proverbs 18:24a; I Corinthians 6:20; Colossians 3:5;
James 4:4b

***See "Abstinence"

Marriage

To get married is an important step!
To love and stay with someone
for the rest of your life!
A promise you'll keep forever with the
One you have chosen to be husband or wife.

You must always put your life-mate first
And with others never flirt.
You must work hard to make your mate feel loved,
Never criticizing or trying to hurt.

God may bless you with a family,
So be a wise mother or dad.
Be good examples to your children
And they will always make your hearts glad!

Marriage is a picture of Christ and His church --
Which time and circumstance can never part!
His love is never-failing and sure --
Let your spouse know your loving heart.

Man: ..."he that is married cares...how he may
please his wife." I Corinthians 7:33
Woman: "...she that is married cares...how she
may please her husband." I Corinthians 7:34

Genesis 2:24; I Corinthians 7:3; Ephesians 5:33;
Hebrews 13:4; I Peter 3:7

***See "Marriage is Forever"

Commitment

The person you will marry
Will live with you the rest of your life.

So do not be satisfied
With someone who'll bring you strife.

You must truly love and serve one another
Always putting the other one first!

Show love and kindness every day
And, together, for God's will greatly thirst.

Read His word and attend a sound church,
Build your lives on His precepts...

God intends your marriage to last until death
So each marriage vow MUST be kept!

"A virtuous woman is a crown to her husband..." Proverbs
24:4; "Every wise woman builds her house."
Proverbs 14:1; "Whoever finds a wife finds a good
thing, and obtains favor of the Lord." Proverbs 18:22
"Through wisdom is an house built; and by
understanding it is established." Proverbs 24:3
"Husbands, love your wives, even as Christ loved the
church and gave himself for it." Ephesians 5:25

Ephesians 5:22,24,28; Colossians 3:18,19;
I Peter 3:7
***See "Marriage is Forever"
"Submission"

Adultery

Adultery means being unfaithful
to the person you have married...
It seems that all the love you had
You have decided to forsake and bury.

You give your affection to somebody else --
One you think you like much more...
Not caring that you have broken the law
and the heart of your partner tore!

God commands that the person you wed
Is to be your partner for life...
Not to be abandoned at your whim (wish)
Or be forsaken because of strife (fighting).

Problems can be solved if properly tackled,
Love for each other can be renewed...
A family of kids should not be abandoned,
Because of your unsolvable feud.

God: "I have loved thee with an everlasting love..."
Jeremiah 31:3a; "With all lowliness and meekness,
with longsuffering, forbearing one another in love,
endeavoring to keep the unity..." Ephesians 4:2,3;
"Wives, submit yourselves unto your own husbands...
husbands, love your wives, and
be not bitter against them." Colossians 3:18,19;

Deuteronomy 19:9a; Proverbs 5:19c;
John 14:15; 15:10; I Peter 1:22b; I John 4:18a; 5:2;
Revelation 2:4 (Christ's example)

Work

Don't tell me you are "lazy!"
And do not like to work!!
If you are, you won't ever succeed (win).
So many dangers lurk (bad things wait).

No-one likes a "shirker" --
Who doesn't really try.
If you don't cooperate -- do your part --
Your friends will pass you by.

Hard work helps you grow,
It's needed to get things done --
And even if you are not paid,
Good friendships you have won!

Work means lots of exercise --
You may even sweat!!
Your body will become strong --
Such satisfaction you will get!

"That ye might walk worthy of the Lord unto all
pleasing, being fruitful in every good work, and
increasing in the knowledge of God." Colossians
1:10; "...study to be quiet, and to do your own
business, and to work with your own hands..."
I Thessalonians 4:11; "...if any would not work,
neither should he eat." II Thessalonians 3:10;
"And whatsoever ye do, do it heartily, as to the
Lord, and not unto men." Colossians 3:23

I Corinthians 3:13; II Corinthians 9:8; Titus 3:1c;
I Peter 1:17

Servants

Did you know there are very many people
Who will help your life to protect?
The policeman on the corner,
When the traffic he directs.
He's also there to keep you safe
From any harm or danger:
From robbery or kidnapping --
And "molestation" by a stranger. (wrong things)

The mailman brings the mail each day,
The librarian finds the books you select (choose).
The fireman risks his very life
Your home and property to protect.

The doctor's there to help you keep well,
Your teacher helps you to read and to spell.
The grocer cares for the food you will eat.
The farmer plows in the rain and the heat!
The "butcher, the baker, the candle-stick maker"
All serve you as best as they can.
Some day, you, too, will be a servant to others.
It's been this way since time began!

꧁꧂

"Whoever will be great among you, let him be your minister:
and whoever will be chief among you, let him be your
servant. Even as the Son of man came not to be
ministered unto but to minister and to give his life
a ransom for many." Matthew 20:26-28

꧁꧂

Proverbs 25:21; Matthew 24:46; Mark 10:43b;
Philippians 4:13; Colossians 1:10;
II Timothy 2:24; Hebrews 13:2a

Appreciation

There are many folk who serve you!
The postman, policeman and firefighter, too.
Your parents, librarians and teachers --
Who do things, unpaid by you.

They give of their time and efforts.
Some may even give up their lives!
But because they perform their daily tasks,
The city and schools can survive. (keep going)

So be sure to appreciate all they do
And thank them when you can.
Some day you may be a servant too
And you'll appreciate every fan!

❦

"(Give) thanks always for all things unto God..."
Ephesians 5:20; "(I) cease not to give thanks...
making mention of you in my prayers." Ephesians 1:16

❦

Matthew 10:10b, 25:21a; Luke 10:7b,
Romans 14:18; Ephesians 4:1b; I Timothy 5:18b

America

We have the finest country

In all of the world today...

You can be proud to be an American.

For its strengths you should daily pray.

We are free to come and go as we please,

To succeed in all that we do...

Never to fear those around us,

To enjoy our vast resources, too!

God has blessed us as we have honored Him

Our country on God's Word was formed.

But today we are seeing many go astray --

So to God's will your own life conform.

"If my people, which are called by my name, shall humble
themselves, and pray, and seek my face, and turn from
their wicked ways; then will I hear from heaven, and
will forgive their sin, and heal their land." II Chronicles 7:14;
"And I brought you into a plentiful country, to eat the fruit...
and the goodness thereof." Jeremiah 2:7a

I Samuel 2:7; Proverbs 10:4; 22:2; I Corinthians
4:8a, I Timothy 6:17-19; I Peter 2:13-17

Our Flag

The flag, our country's symbol,
With its colors -- red, white and blue,
Should have a special meaning
That speaks to the heart of you.

It represents the freedoms
That all in our country know...
Fought for by brave men and women
Who've conquered our every foe.

The stars and stripes are beautiful to see,
As in the sky they proudly fly.
Every man and boy should remove his hat,
All should stand when the flag passes by.

You must give it proper respect,
Let it fly proud and free.
Respect and never betray it,
Let all your allegiance see!

"Lift ye up a banner upon the high mountain."
Isaiah 13:2a

Proverbs 3:27; Romans 8:21+

Diversity

There are people of different races
That are a part of America today,

Their skins are of different colors
And their speech not like words we say.

But we must treat them all as neighbors
And try to accept them, one and all.

For ours is a land of freedom --
And each one a "patriot"* we call.
(*person who loves his country)

We must try to understand their feelings
And do our best to be a friend.
This will unite our country
And help its liberties (freedoms) to defend.

"Behold, how good and how pleasant it is for brethren
to dwell together in unity!" Psalm 133:1
"Be kindly affectionate one to another with brotherly
love; in honor preferring one another." Romans 12:10

Genesis 11:7,8a (when man wanted to be in control)

Holy Spirit

Do you know you've someone to help you?
Who lives within your heart
to help you do right
and from the Lord not to depart?

He'll teach you as you read His Word,
Help against Satan to fight.
He will guide your steps
And keep you walking aright.

Be careful not to spurn (forget) Him --
Forget to ask for his aid (help).
Listen for His still, small voice
Of your foes (enemies) you'll not be afraid.

"He...hath given us his Holy Spirit." I Thessalonians 4:8;
"...there are three that bear record in heaven, the
Father, the Word, and the Holy Ghost: and these
three are one." I John 5:7; "Quench not the
Spirit." I Thessalonians 5:19

Galatians 5:22,23; Ephesians 4:30; I Thessalonians
1:6; II Timothy 1:14; Titus 3:5; Hebrews 2:4;
I Peter 1:12; II Peter 1:21

Saints

Every Christian is called a "saint"
Who to God can directly pray--
(Not just those whom the church calls great)
And can help others not to stray.

All Christians are in favor with God
And to others a blessing can be --

But, after death, they cannot grant favors --
Pray you into Heaven for a fee!

As saints, we CAN pray for others --
This is a privilege we own.

But only for earthly blessing --
Not after leaving earth's zone!

❧❧

"Precious in the sight of the Lord is the death of His
saints." Psalm 116:15; "Unto the church of God which
is in Corinth, to them that are sanctified in Christ Jesus,
called to be saints, with all that call upon the name
of Jesus Christ, our Lord." I Corinthians 1:2

❧❧

Psalm 31:23a; 85:8b; Proverbs 2:8; Zechariah
14:5d; Romans 8:27; 16:15; II Corinthians 13:13;
Ephesians 2:19; 5:3

Idols

God forbids worshiping idols --
Or anything to represent Him make!
He alone has wisdom and power --
All other 'gods' are just plain fake!!

But people bow down and serve them --
Yet they cannot even serve on their own!
They sit on shoulders or are carried --
Made of wood or gems or stone.

There is only one true God
Who created the heavens and earth.
He alone can answer one's prayers
And give man a "second birth."

There are other idols not made of stone --
Some worship people, places or things...
But our God is a jealous God
And great condemnation this brings.

❧

"Turn ye not to idols, nor make to yourself molten
gods: I am the Lord your God." Leviticus 19:4;
"...ye have seen their...idols, wood and stone,
silver and gold." Deuteronomy 29:17; "...they
served idols...the Lord had said unto them,
Ye shall not do this thing." II Kings 17:12

❧

II Kings 17:12; 21:20,21; II Chronicles 15:8; Psalm
96:5; 106:36; 115:4-8; Isaiah 2:8; Habakkuk 3:18;
I John 5:21

God's Will

God has a wonderful plan for you!
He wants for you His very best --

But He does not force you to obey
Yet, if you do, you WILL be blessed!

If you follow His plan for your life,
You will know real joy and peace,

You may not be rich in this world's goods
But from anxiety, find release.

If you daily pray to do His will,
He will show you the way to go --

To give Him first place in our life,
His guidance and peace you will know!

❧❧

"Remember now thy Creator in the days of thy
youth..." Ecclesiastes 12:1a; "I will say of the Lord, He
is my refuge and my fortress: my God; in Him will I trust."
Psalm 91:2; "Because he hath set his love upon me,
therefore will I deliver him: I will set him on high,
because he hath known my name. He shall call upon me,
and I will answer him: I will be with him in trouble: I will
deliver him and honor him." Psalm 91:14-16

❧❧

Psalm 31:15a; 48:14; 56:11; 63:1a; 84:11; 101:3a;
118:6; 119:15, 47, 93a, 121:8; I Corinthians 6:12;
Ephesians 6:7; Colossians 3:2; I Thessalonians
5:18; I Timothy 2:12

Missionaries

God has chosen those of His own

To take His word around the globe --

He may call you to leave your home,

Even ask you to suffer, like Job.

But, be assured He has promised to go

To the ends of the world with you --

If you are obedient, He will guide

And treasure in Heaven will endue.

He has promised "never to leave you"

So you can go anywhere He may lead.

Knowing that He will give you the strength

And supply your every need.

꙳ꙅ꙳

"And the gospel of the kingdom shall be preached
in all the world for a witness unto all nations."
Matthew 24:14a; "I will never leave you or
forsake you." Hebrews 13:5c

꙳ꙅ꙳

Isaiah 6:8; Matthew 9:37,38; 28:19,20;
Mark 13:10; Luke 21:28

***See "Serving"

Creation

Do you ever lie in bed and wonder...How did I get here?
How can I do all the things I can? Why are there so many
people? Who made the earth, the seas, the mountains,
the clouds and all that I know? The only answer is found
in God's Word (the Bible)! It tells us that He made the
heavens and the earth. He alone made the mountains,
sends millions of snowflakes...And best of all, creates
men and animals through birth!

No, we cannot fully understand Him and how He did
all these things...We must accept them by faith and in
His power believe. To think that everything just
"happened" Is how Satan wants to deceive. The parts
of a watch could lay on a table for millions and millions
of years! But they would never come together to
become a watch, that's un-contradictable and clear!

To believe in God and His Son, the Creator,
guarantees you will forever live! How foolish to
question His power and love. -- What future does any
other belief give? God is All-Powerful -- anything's
possible for Him! He has a purpose and plan for you!
Give Him the honor that He deserves
And you will KNOW all the answers that are true!

"In the beginning, God made the heavens and the earth."
Genesis 1:1; "Lift up your eyes on high, and behold who
hath created these things..." Isaiah 40:26; "I have made
the earth, and created man upon it..." Isaiah 45:12

Genesis 1, Isaiah 40:28; Ecclesiastes 2:1;
Ephesians 3:9; Colossians 1:16

***See: "Countless"

Evolution

Some believe that we evolved (came) from
apes (monkeys).
Which, according to the Bible, is not true.
God is the One Who created (made) ALL things!
We must give Him the credit (trust) that is due.

They say that the earth is millions of years old!
But the Bible (God's Word) says this isn't so.
God created (made) everything in seven days --
Which isn't "hard" for Him, you know.

It took a mind so wonderful to plan everything we know!
They did not "just happen" like they say...
Men are just guessing, judging by what they think --
But attention to their ideas we must not pay!

God can even make something new look old!!
And everything He made man cannot duplicate--
(do the same) --
They do not want to acknowledge their Maker
(admit He exists) --
Or that to the earth their Savior came!

"In the beginning, God made the heavens and the earth."
Genesis 1:1; "...ask now of the days that are past, which
were before thee, since the day that God created man
upon the earth..." Deuteronomy 4:32; "Lift up your eyes on
high, and behold who hath created these things...who calls
them all by names...not one fails." Isaiah 40:26 "I have made
the earth, and created man upon it...stretched out the heavens,
and all their host have I commanded." Isaiah 45:12

GENESIS 1
Isaiah 40:28; Ecclesiastes 12:1; Isaiah 40:28;
Ephesians 3:9; Colossians 1:16

Angels

The angels are God's helpers,
They obey His every command.
You probably have one in charge of you
And are protected by their hand.

Good angels war against Satan --
And many evil (bad) ones are on his side,
Joining "The Evil One" rebelling against God
Because of their undeserved pride.

Good angels constantly praise God
And serve Him day and night.
They are present all over the world.
You can never be out of their sight.

When God decides to destroy the world,
The angels will do all He asks.
They are so strong and mighty
And can perform God's hardest tasks!

We who are saved will join them
To praise God eternally,
For all the blessings He's promised
To bestow on you and me!

❧❧

"In the beginning God created the heavens and the earth."
Genesis 1:1 "Of old hath thou laid the foundation of the earth:
and the heavens are the work of thy hands." Psalm 102:25;
"He causes the vapors to ascend from the ends of the earth;
he makes lightning for the rain; he brings the wind out of
his treasuries." Psalm 135:7 "The heavens declare the glory
of God; and the firmament shows his handiwork." Psalm 19:1

❧❧

Psalm 24:1; 33:5b; 69:34; 90:2; 136:5-9; 147:4; Proverbs
3:19; Ecclesiastes 3:14; Colossians 1:16,17

Satan

Do you know who is your greatest enemy?
Who always wants you to do wrong?
He tries to make you disobey God --
He and his demons try all day long!

The Bible says he can be like a lion
Or he can be as gentle as a sheep.
Beware of all his tricks --
Don't let him catch you asleep!

Jesus has more power than the devil,
He already beat him at the Cross.
You must always count on His help.
He rewards those who let Him be boss!

So, watch out for all Satan's traps.
How do you defeat him? -- by prayer!
Satan will flee (run) with God on your side --
But you must ask God to be there.

"And the Lord said, Simon (Peter), ...Satan hath desired
to have you..." Luke 22:31; "...lest Satan should get an
advantage of us..." II Corinthians 2:11a "...Satan himself is
transformed into an angel of light." II Corinthians 11:14; "Jesus
said ...get thee behind me, Satan..." Luke 4:8; "To open their
eyes, and to turn them from darkness to light, and from the
power of Satan unto God..." Acts 26:18a; "Submit yourselves...
to God, Resist the devil, and he will flee from you." James 4:7;
I Peter 5:8: "Be...vigilant, because your adversary, the devil,
as a roaring lion, walks about, seeking whom he may
devour." I Peter 5:8

I John 3:8a

Sin

Sin is anything you do
That displeases God above.
But even though you sin,
He does not exclude (keep you away)
from His love!
Adam, the first man God created,
Chose God's commands to disobey
So everyone inherited this sin --
EVERYONE living on earth today!

But you do not have to STAY a sinner!
God made a way to forgive you.
Jesus, His Son, took your place
And paid the penalty that was due!!

But you must ask for forgiveness
And accept His gift so free --
He will help you live for Him,
An obedient child to be!

❧❧

"Blessed is he whose transgression (sin) is covered..."
Psalm 32:1b: "For I will declare my iniquity: I will be
sorry for my sin." Psalm 3818; "Thy word have I hid in
mine heart, that I might not sin against thee." Psalm
119:11; "For the wages of sin is death; but the gift of
God is eternal life through Jesus Christ our Lord."
Romans 6:23; "He hath made him to be sin for us,
who knew no sin; that we might be made the
righteousness of God in Him." II Corinthians 5:21

❧❧

Psalm 4:4; 39:1a; 51:2, 3; 119:11; Proverbs 14:9a;
Romans 3:20b; 5:12, 20; 6:2,12, 23; 14:23b;
Galatians 3:22; Ephesians 4:26,27;
Hebrews 11:25; James 2:9a; I John 1:5; 2:1

Temptation

Satan appears as an "angel of light"
As he tempts men to be on his side.
But he is really a roaring lion --
And into wicked habits he will guide.

So, beware, of all his well-set traps --
Don't fall for his slippery ways.
If you yield your body to Christ each day
He will keep you from going astray.

You can set an example for others
By living for Christ alone...
You can help your sisters and brothers
If, by a pure life, you are known.

Don't smoke or drink or gamble
Go along with a wicked (wrong) plan...
God will honor you if you resist (don't),
And, with His great help, you can!!

❦

"Flee also youthful lusts: but follow righteousness,
faith, charity, peace" II Timothy 2:22; "Neither
yield your members as instruments of unrighteousness
unto sin: but yield yourselves unto God, as those
that are alive from the dead, and your members as
instruments of righteousness unto God." Romans 6:13,

❦

Romans 6:16,19; II Corinthians 11:14; II Timothy 2:26;
Hebrews 4:15; James 1:12; II Peter 2:9a

Atheists

There are people in America
That want to shut God out of our land!
They do not acknowledge His loving care
That gave us our freedoms so grand.

They would erase many of our age-old customs –
Get rid of Christmas and Easter, too.
They want to eliminate any mention of God
In our government and even our schools.

They do not honor God as creator
But think that man just evolved!
Instead of seven days (of which God is able!)
They think Evolution their problem solves.

How foolish to deny the very One
Who gave them their very life!
They forfeit their future life with Him –
And nurture much confusion and strife!

"Consider my enemies; for they are many.
and they hate me with cruel hatred." Psalm 25:19;
"...they hated knowledge and did not choose the
fear of the Lord." Proverbs 1:29; "If the world
hate you, ye know that it hated me before it hated
you." John 15:18

Psalm 38:20; John 17:14

Old Age

Some day you may be old
And your hair may turn gray.
Perhaps you'll walk with a cane,
Take naps during the day.

You may not hear as well,
Have glasses to help you see.
You may be stooped over –
And very forgetful be.

So I hope you'll not make fun,
For oldsters are very wise.
They've learned a lot of things –
They're "treasures" in disguise.

Please try to be extra kind
And listen carefully.
Let them share their stories –
And you will wiser be!

"Cast me not off in the time of old age, forsake
me not when my strength fails." Psalm 71:9;.
"…Days should speak, and multitude of years
should teach wisdom." Job 32:7;
"You should rise up before the hoary head, and
know the face of the old man, and fear thy God."
Leviticus 19:32

Psalm 92:14a; Titus 2:2,3

Alzheimer's

In later life, this may happen to you...
Well-known habits will begin to change,
You may start to forget what day it is
And may put things in places strange!

Your favorite stories you will repeat and repeat,
And your facts will not always be right.
You may look and look for well-known things
When they are not really "out of sight."

You may become dangerous to others,
Your drivers' license they may take
For you'll be considered "accident-prone" --
Your foot on the accelerator instead of the brake!

You may wander away from your home
And not have a clue where you are --
You may become afraid to be alone,
For Alzheimer's your life will mar (hurt).

Life is like a grain of sand
Compared to Eternity!
How foolish to concentrate
On things that will cease to be!

❧❧❧

"There is no remembrance of former things..."
Ecclesiastes 1:11a; "...call to remembrance the
former days..." Hebrews 10:32a; "You should
rise up before the hoary head, and honor the
face of the old man..." Leviticus 19:32a;
"The hoary head is a crown of glory, if it be
found in the way of righteousness." Proverbs 16: 31

Death

This is something we don't like to talk about,
When our bodies are laid in a grave.

What happens when our lives are over?
Can we face this and still be brave?

The Christian does not have to fear death...
For we will live to be with God!

He will greet us when we breathe our last breath,
Just our bodies will stay in the sod (ground).

Christ is coming back in the sky one day --
In all His glory He will appear!

If alive, He will take us Home to be with Him,
And that day may be very near.

❧

"Whether...the world, or life, or death, or things
present, or things to come, all are yours; and
you are Christ's; and Christ is God's."
I Corinthians 3:22,23; "Death is swallowed up
in victory." I Corinthians 15:54b

❧

Philippians 1:20, 21; I John 3:14a

***See "Marathon of Life"

Funerals

When you attend (go to) a funeral,
Remember, the person in the coffin
Is no longer there --
If a Christian, they're up in Heaven,
God's Home forever to share.

It's just their "left-over" body
Who you visit with respect (love),
Whom friends and loved ones honor
And give comfort in time of stress.
(a hard time)

There will be beautiful flowers
And photos of the family to see --
And you must mind your manners (how you act)
A "gentleman" or "lady" you must be!

Listen to the nice things said,
And the "guest book" you may sign --
They will put the body in the ground,
To rise up at a future time.

A new body will be given
That forever then will live...
To enjoy the God Who made us --
Thanks to Jesus in love to give!

❧❧

"Precious in the sight of the Lord is the death of
his saints." Psalm 116:15; "He will swallow up death
in victory, and the Lord God will wipe away all tears...
Isaiah 25:8a; "...while we are at home in the body, we
are absent from the Lord." II Corinthians 5:6b

❧❧

Romans 8:38; I Corinthians 3:32; 15:26, 52-57;
II Timothy 2:11; I John 3:14

The Rapture

The rapture is a special event
That all Christians are waiting for...
When Jesus comes back to earth again
And all Christians to Heaven will soar!

All those who are dead and buried
Will rise up to meet the Lord first.
Then the Christians who are still alive
Up into the heavens will burst!

Those on earth who rejected the Lord
Will think this is a mystery --
People have vanished and cars have crashed --
Things unexplained come to be!

To be a part of this exit so grand,
You MUST belong to God's family --
Since your sins have been forgiven,
Your home in Heaven will be!

"I would not have you ignorant...concerning them which are
asleep, that ye sorrow not, as those who have no hope...
the Lord himself shall descend from heaven...the dead in
Christ shall rise first; then we which are alive...shall be
caught up...to meet the Lord in the air; and so shall we ever
be with the Lord." I Thessalonians 4:13-18
"...ye...are not in darkness, that that day should overtake
you as a thief." I Thessalonians 5:4

Titus 2:13; II Peter 3:10-12

Heaven

Heaven is a wonderful place
But not everyone will go there!

You must know Christ as your Savior,
Your complete faith in Him declare.

Heaven is never-ending --
A place where you will never die.
You will have a brand-new body --
Your every need God will supply.

No sickness or sadness,
No fighting or war.
Tame will be all the animals --
Not a thing to wish for!

I hope I will see you in Heaven --
You can tell me if you liked my book!
I hope it has helped you very much.
For YOU I will surely look!!

"...we know that all things work together for good to them
that love God, to them who are the called according
to His purpose." Romans 8:28

Romans 8:17,18; 38:39; I Corinthians 2:9; Hebrews
11:16; Ephesians 2:6,7; Colossians 1:5a;
Hebrews 9:24; 11:16a; Revelation 22

Anti-christ

At some time in the future,
A sinister (evil) man will rule the world --
He will hate God and try to imitate Him,
And then God's wrath (anger) will be unfurled!
(let loose)

He will be against all the Jewish people.
God's chosen ones he will chase and kill!
Yet now there will be many of them
That believe God's Word is being fulfilled.

Thousands of them their lives will lose!
But forty-four thousand will be saved --
To enjoy Heaven with their Maker
And forever give their Lord praise!!

The world will know untold disasters (horrible things),
People for their lives will flee!
But Christ, His angels and all Christians will fight
and the Anti-Christ's defeat will see!!

"For in those days shall be affliction, such as was
not from the beginning of the creation...neither
shall be." Mark 13:19-29
"...anti-Christ shall come...whereby we know
that it is the last time." I John 2:18

Daniel 8:19;
II Timothy 3:1; I John 2:22

Judgment

Some day God will judge the world --
To rid the world of its sin.
He will send all sinners to Hell
But not those who've invited the Savior in.

Jesus died that we might live
FOREVER with Him above...
HEAVEN IS your destiny
Where nothing is known but love.

Be sure you make your choice very soon
For Jesus might come today!
You would not want to be "left behind" --
For your sins you would have to pay.

"...He cometh to judge the earth: he shall judge
the world with righteousness, and the people with
his truth." Psalms 96:13b; "The day of the Lord
will come as a thief in the night...seeing that all
...things shall be dissolved, what manner of persons
ought ye to be..." II Peter 3:10,11

Luke 6:37; Romans 1:16; I Corinthians 6:2a;
I Thessalonians 5:2; II Thessalonians 1:7-10;
II Timothy 4:1; I Peter 3:22
II Peter 3:10

God's Agenda

Do you know God's plans for the future?
Or in your mind, are they blurred?

When you know them well, you will not fear
For the Christian, God's love is assured.

If you've asked the Lord to forgive your sin,
You'll be spared from all the trouble ahead.
There'll come great tribulation for the Jews,
And the world, by the Anti-Christ led.

He is Satan's man to deceive all mankind
But God's mighty army will prevail.
Then Christ will rule the world with love
And His plans will never fail.
After the Millennium, a thousand years,
God will send all the wicked to Hell.
But the Christian will live forever,
God's loving goodness to tell!

"...eye hath not seen, nor ear heard, neither have
entered into the heart of man, the things which
God hath prepared for them that love Him."
I Corinthians 2:9; "Whosoever believeth in Him
should not perish, but have eternal life." John 3:15

Matthew 24:21; Revelation 20, 21, 22

Schedule of Future Events

1. CHRIST'S SECOND RETURN -- IN THE AIR!
No-one except God knows when this will happen.
Jesus will return to earth just like He left -- in the
clouds! The Christians who have died will rise
from their graves and the Christians who are
still alive will join them in the air.
WE WILL ALL GO TO HEAVEN
TOGETHER!
We will have new bodies and live with Jesus!
I Thessalonians 4:15-17

2.   THE GREAT TRIBULATION (7 YEARS)
While we are gone, the JEWISH PEOPLE on
earth will suffer great trouble under the reign of the
ANTI-CHRIST.
He takes over the world and claims to BE Christ.
He is a fake but the world then will believe him and
the Jewish people, whom God chose to be His
long ago, will finally realize that Jesus is God and
144,000 of them will now believe and be saved.
Matthew 24:21; II Thessalonians 2:3,4;
Revelation 7:4

3. ALL CHRISTIANS WILL BE JUDGED
while the TRIBULATION is happening on earth.
NOT FOR SINS WE HAVE COMMITTED
BUT
FOR THINGS WE HAVE DONE FOR CHRIST
during our lifetimes. II Corinthians 5:10
GOD WILL REWARD US WITH CROWNS
IF WE WERE FAITHFUL AND OBEDIENT.
II TIMOTHY 4:8; I Peter 5:4

(Continued)

4. WHEN THE TRIBULATION IS OVER:
CHRIST AND ALL HIS SAINTS (that's US!)
WILL RETURN TO EARTH AND WAR
AGAINST THE ANTI-CHRIST AND HIS
ARMIES – AND CONQUER HIM!
I Thessalonians 3:13

5. CHRIST WILL BE OUR RULER ON EARTH FOR 1,000 YEARS! And WE SHALL REIGN WITH HIM and FOR HIM.
II Timothy 2:12; Revelation 5:10

6. THE GREAT WHITE THRONE JUDGMENT
When **ALL THE UNSAVED PEOPLE** will be
punished – because they did not choose to
accept God's free gift of salvation and lived
their lives for themselves, constantly sinning
against God – Revelation 20:11-15
**They will be CAST INTO HELL FOREVER
Along with SATAN and
ALL WICKED ANGELS**

7. WE WILL LIVE FOREVER WITH GOD AND JESUS! There will be a **NEW HEAVEN AND NEW EARTH.** We will live on both,
Serving God and enjoying everything beautiful
NO MORE SIN, SICKNESS, EVIL OR DEATH!

(Continued)

8. HEAVEN: A PLACE WITH NO NEED OF THE SUN, FOR GOD IS LIGHT!

The Holy City will have streets paved with
GOLD and fruit trees that bear fruit all year
long. We will KNOW EVERYONE:
MOSES, KING DAVID, SOLOMON AND
ALL of our SAVED RELATIVES.
Everyone will be kind and loving.
The animals will not kill each other.
Children can even play with lions and
spiders!
God will give us everything good that
We can enjoy and do and…
THIS WILL NEVER END!
Isaiah 11:6-9; Revelation 22:1-5

+++++

BE SURE YOU ARE ONE THAT WILL BE READY WHEN CHRIST RETURNS FOR HIS OWN!

Abstinence
The Only Way That Works!

Teenagers, please give heed
To what you are about to read.
Sex is the only God-ordained way
to populate the earth.
To "go all the way"
is asking your Creator to bring about a birth.

Then, to abandon that baby in the womb,
Propelling it to certain doom,
Is a wrong decision, now made twice,
And with it comes an awesome price.
There follows a never-ending guilt,
Makes it hard for future family to be built.
Satan is your formidable foe,
Refrain from lust, God will help you say, "No!"

One need not, then, fear painful disease
Or be given a "second-hand" love.
The marriage bed is worth the waiting,
It's the God-given reward for legitimate dating.
You'll reap true happiness and genuine love,
Life-long blessings from your Father above.

ABORTION
A finished story?
A closed tale?
No
You have just "shut the book" --
The story is still there,
Never to be read!

All Of Life

Worship is not just for Sunday morn,
but should permeate our lives...

To keep the Lord foremost in our thoughts,
we should more actively strive.

The words that we say and things we do,
His wise approval should meet --

Daily our first fervent prayer should be
that He alone guide our feet.

We can worship with deeds of kindness
to those we find in great need.

We also worship with joyful song
as His Word we daily read.

When raising our youth to know the Truth,
disciplining tenderly...

We make sure our children do not stray,
as Christ in our lives they see!

We worship God with all of our life --
each moment and every hour.

But true worship can never be known
without the Spirit's power!

A Toddler's Prayers

"God is great and God is good,"
Is a favorite toddlers pray --
It's often said at dinnertime
but added to through the day...

''Help my froggy not to die"
"Please help grandpa to get well,"
"Make my tummy-ache go 'way"
And "See my hurt knee, where I fell."

Nothing is too big or small
for their Father up above.
They seem to sense His wisdom
and trust His unfailing love!

Prayer Project

Find a special stone or rock in your garden or on the
beach. Then do this to help you to remember to pray.

❧☙

"I'm a little prayer rock and this is what I'll do: Just put me
on your pillow until the day is through. Then turn back the
covers and climb into bed and WHACK! Your little prayer
rock will hit you on the head! Then you will remember
just as the day is through to kneel and say your prayers,
as you really wanted to. Then after you are finished, just
drop me on the floor. I'll stay there through the night, time to
give you help once more. When you get up the next morning,
CLUNK! I'll stub your toe, so you'll remember your
morning prayers before you go! Put me back upon your
pillow when your bed is made, and your little rock will continue
to aid...because your heavenly Father cares and loves you so.
He wants you to remember to talk to Him, you know.
--Author unknown

Be Involved

Each child of God has a place in the church

that no-one else can fill.

And each must offer his service to God,

determining and obeying His will.

❧❧

It is He Who enables with talents and health

and you'll be amazed at what HE can do

if you surrender to Him your time and wealth --

He can accomplish so much through you!

So do not sit back and watch others work

but pitch in and do your share.

May the church be a place

where no-one will shirk,

each helping the burden to bear.

Big Or Little?

Which does God use more...
The gigantic or the small?
Who best can gain the victory,
To make a giant fall?

Does He need a horde of soldiers,
With swords and armor clad?
No, God can use one volunteer...
As when David was a lad!

Does he need a mighty army
To rout a powerful foe?
No, God can triumph with a handful
As Gideon came to know!

Does He need a score of messengers
To warn when dangers loom?
No, Jonah preached to Nineveh
And saved a nation from doom!

When leading His chosen people
To the distant Promised Land...
Moses and Aaron were the two who led
This multitudinous band!

(Continued)

Did God need countless angels
To rescue man from his sin?
No, His only Son was the chosen One
To woo mankind back to Him!

So, we see that God is seen to work
Through people and things quite small...
We must be willing, though unimportant and weak,
To always be "on call."

If going forth in our own strength alone,
All our efforts will come to naught!
But by letting God have His way in our lives,
Our battles are already fought...

The victory is His, for He is the One
Who works on our behalf...
He sits on His throne in the Heavens above
And over the "mighty" He laughs!

Come Sailing With Me!

I don't have to wait

Until I am a man

Places far to see,

Like China or Japan.

I have many ships

That sail the seven seas.

I need pay no fare,

I board them as I please.

I can tour the world,

At wonders I can look.

Have you guessed my ships?

I sail in every book!

Comprehending God

Comprehend God? Never! Not with our mortal minds --
The more one contemplates His attributes,
the greater the mysteries one finds!
He knows the end from the beginning
and nothing takes Him by surprise --
His holiness defies description and in Him all truth lies.

We cannot fathom His creative powers
and marvel at all that He's made --
The variety of things, both great and small,
how precisely the universe is laid!

Every need of man is met and animal
life is sustained --
The order of the seasons and time,
all by His mind ordained!
How He can exist with no beginning or end,.
who or what created Him?
We who are bound by time and space
find our earthly vision so dim!

We know that man is made in His image
and thus a part of Him we can know
But to pinpoint His every facet is
impossible here below,
Someday, those who love Him down here
will join Him in Heaven above
And He will reveal Himself to His own --
to those who have accepted His love.

Even harder to understand is His acceptance of us
who have ruined this world with our sin!
This, I'm afraid, we will never digest--
even though Eternity we win.

Dare!

by Granddaughter
KAITLYN ELIZABETH SCHONTA
- Age 11 -

D is for DRUG,
which makes you a slug!
A is for ABUSE,
which is simply "misuse."
R is for RESISTANCE,
which means to "keep away!"
E's for EDUCATION,
which teaches the way to stay.
DRU-U-UG FREE!
is the way to be.
Keeping your self-esteem high
is the key.
DRU-U-UG FREE!
is the way for me.
I don't want to hurt my life or family.
Think through all the consequences carefully
Before making a choice.
Listen to your inner voice.
Don't get frantic or too stressed,
Just make the decision you KNOW is best.

Don't Let Go!

He will walk hand in hand with you
Through the paths of this new day --

You will feel the warmth of his gentle grip
And your feet will not go astray.

For He'll be at your side
To expertly guide
Or support when weakened or tired...

And when trouble you meet,
He will lift your feet
And carry you over the mire.

If you stumble or fall,
He will hear your call
And immediate comfort you'll know,

So reach out today
For the Savior's strong hand---
It is you, not He, that let's go!

Do We Think We Know It All?

How much of this world's knowledge
Do you think that we possess?
A mere teaspoon of its ocean,
We must truthfully confess.
Have we read the billions of books
that countless authors have penned?
To every nook and cranny on earth
did our extensive travels send?

Can our minds explain the intricacies
of every invention of man?
If so, we could spawn quite a few
and improve on some, if we can.
Do we really know from what we were made,
how our minds and bodies function?
If we do, we would become physical czars --
We'd deserve that grandiose unction!

Do you now agree that what we know is miniscule
and what we don't know, far greater?
Then somewhere, within that vast unknown,
there could be an All-Wise Creator?
How He came to be and possess such power
is beyond comprehension...
But that He exists may be certain fact,
not subject to man's condescension.

(Continued)

And, if we could explain His existence
and the wonders of His creations,
Then we would possess all the knowledge on earth,
God would need no validation!
He's bestowed on man His highest form of life,
and many of His own attributes --
The mind is one, with which to think
but not for His Being to refute!
And in man alone, He has implanted a soul
that can reach the Heavenly plane.
If one possesses God's Spirit within,
some day, knowledge of ALL he will gain!

Dumping!

<u>D</u> is for DROPPING THINGS

all through the house!

(Turning your neat momma into a grouse!)

<u>U</u> is for the UGLY SCENE it makes.

<u>M</u> is for the more CLEAN-UP time it takes.

<u>P</u> is for the PLACE everything should be --

And DUMP

is the name of the mess you see!

୧ॐ୭

Clothes can be worn twice
if not left in a heap,

And a well-made bed
makes for more restful sleep.

No need to worry, then, if friends 'drop in' --
Your room will ALWAYS
be as neat as a pin!

୧ॐ୭

DON'T DUMP!!

I Don't Want A 'Grumpy' Grandma!

When I go to Grandma's house,

I play with all her toys!

And she doesn't seem to mind it

If I make a lot of noise.

❧❦☙

Well, she always seems to know

just when I need a treat --

And ice cream and a cookie

is what I like to eat!

❧❦☙

So when I leave my Grandma's house,

I pick up every game --

I don't want my Grandma sad

but happy that I came!

I Ran Away From Home!

I ran away from home yesterday,

I really wasn't angry, just bored!

I didn't take my backpack with me

And couldn't have cared less if it poured!

I wanted to get as far away
As I could from my little brother!

And I didn't want to be close by,
Answering questions from my mother!

I wanted to be all by myself

And go somewhere really exciting,

Where no-one would tell me what to do

And lessons I would not be writing!

I would see the world and make brand-new friends

And stay there just as long as it took --

I ran away from home yesterday
to my own secret place --

WITH A BOOK!

Luxuries

I'm thankful for a hamburger,
For a chocolate candy treat.
When many in other lands
Can't find enough to eat!

For stores where I can purchase
Almost any item I wish
While those across the ocean
don't even know what they miss!

I'm thankful for hospital beds
and for tender, loving care,
for some suffer untold pain
with none their grief to share.

I'm thankful for a light bulb!
that gives light to aid in my tasks.
Many lie down when the sun sets,
warm beds and heat they do lack.

I'm thankful for my family
that does not have to fear death --
not waiting for invasion
that might deny their next breath!

The wealth of daily blessings
that I know every day
may never be known by millions --
May I be thankful, Lord, I pray!

Marriage Is Forever

A trip down the aisle to the altar
To declare your love for one another
Requires a promise to live your days
Giving preference one to the other.

Wedding bands given are a token
Of pledges to be faithful and true.
A promise never to be broken
That binds your partner forever to you.

Divorce should not enter the picture
For love should not die but faithfully grow –
If lives are committed to the Lord,
His blessing and love they'll come to know.

Each must work to MAKE the marriage work!
To be worthy and earn their partner's love,
To exhibit God's love at all times,
To please their Heavenly Father above.

'Tis a picture of Christ and His church
Whom He's chosen to be His loving bride.
He pledges His presence forever
And will never ever cast us aside!

My Car

My car goes where I want it to go,
It digests whatever I put into it!
It rests when I park it in the garage --
I repair it, when needed, to keep it fit.
I try to keep it clean and neat,
I take it for routine check-ups...
I make sure it follows the rules of the road,
But sometimes my peace of mind it disrupts!
When a headlight goes out or brake-shoes grow thin,
I must find the time to repair --
Sometimes to the garage it must go
When to trust my own mind, I don't dare!
When others disregard my presence
And cause a dent or accident...
I must count on my insurance
And my innocence present!
When in trouble, I must identify
That the vehicle belongs to me...
For the one who oversees the offense
Has authority my license to see!

My body, too, takes plenty of care...
But is usually under my control.
I feed it what I want to
And it takes me where I want to go!
The amount of rest is up to me...
And cleanliness should be a must!
When hurting, to the doctor I repair...
To one who is worthy of trust.
At times there are those who would annoy
And threaten the peace in my life...
And I must rely on a higher authority,
To straighten out conflict and strife.
My Heavenly Father owns the title to me
And instructs me on how I should run!
If I follow faithfully His "rules of the road,"
I'll resemble the model...HIS SON!

My Prayer

Kaitlyn Elizabeth Schonta
(Age 12)

DEAR GOD:

Bless my parents
and my brothers
and the food I have to eat.
Help me conquer all life's problems
and keep me on my feet.

Help me not to worry
but put my trust in You.
Be by my side to guide me
in all I say and do.
Help me to try my hardest
and do my very best.
Please help me and be with me
through each and every test.

Help me to forgive others,
as you've forgiven me.
And when I do not know the way,
Help me, God, to see.
Thank you, God, for hearing
my each and every call,
And thank you for sending
Your only Son to earth
to save us all.
Amen

My Riches

I am richer than all my worldly friends --
Far surpassing their earthly goods!
They could question my boastful statement
and my meaning be misunderstood.
My treasure exists in the Heavenly clime,
Laid away for a future day --
It can never, ever be stolen from me
or burned or washed away!

The Christian is admonished to work
but not for earthly gain --
Solely for things that cannot fail,
that will forever remain!
"Only what's done for Christ will last,"
so live for Him I must.
Doing the thing that pleases God,
not for my pleasure or lust.

In serving God, I am truly blest,
I don't forfeit any good things
for He chooses to give me His best
and causes my heart to sing.
I AM richer than all my worldly friends
for their goods shall all pass away.
I am a joint-heir with God's own Son
and my treasure is programmed to stay!
The amazing fact of all I possess
is that it's a gift that's free --
It's received from the loving Hand of God
with a tag on it labeled for ME!
And, best of all, it's available to you
if you seek to do His will --
He'll fill your life with blessing right now
and your heavenly treasure-house fill!

Night Light

In bed, a child's fears
may rise to great height

Until Mother comes in
and turns on the light!

The dark is dispelled --
(its visions of doom)

Illumination
now fills the black room!

୶ଈଈ

Fearful is the heart
that knows only night

Until Jesus comes in,
shedding love's bright light!

Dark sin is erased
and wrongs changed to right.

"Turn on" the Bible,
God's faithful
'night light.'

Paying Attention

Do we pay attention, give a "listening ear?"
Are we careful to absorb all the words we need to hear?

The SOLDIER at "Attention!"
must halt and upright stand --
Facing his company officer,
to obey his every command.
And, if he fails to hear aright,
not following the battle plan...
Not only does he suffer
but also his countryman!

A STUDENT must hear his teacher
and listen his very best
if he is to gain the knowledge
that will aid in all life's tests.

The ATHLETE needs to heed his coach,
to play as he's directed...
The outcome of the game being played
is subsequently affected!

(Continued)

A DRIVER, speeding down the road,
must of signals be aware --
Drowsiness or carelessness can cause
the worst nightmare!

How important for the PILOT
to heed weather and control tower --
He cannot let thoughts wander
but must concentrate through each hour!

The PARAMEDIC, FIREMAN and/or NURSE
must pay the strictest of attention --
If they know not what to do, they are
useless for intervention.
And so, we Christians, must listen and obey
the precepts of God's Word --
So as not to miss God's promised rewards,
just because His voice was not heard!

Prayer Is...

PRAYER - A QUIET BREATH
that from my heart I wend
Heavenward --to the One Who said
"Come, your broken life I'll mend."

PRAYER - A COMMUINION SWEET
with the One Who desires to hear
and never tires my soul to meet --
His Presence is always near!

PRAYER - THE TRUE EXPRESSION
of my praise or deepest need.
When God can make an impression
and reveal His Word to heed.

PRAYER - A NEEDFUL TIME OF REST
from the pressures of the day,
A time of calm and renewed zest
as on Christ's bosom I lay.

Race Track

Gambling is an addiction.
It so easily ensnares a man.
Winning is so elusive,
The greedy must win all he can!

He tries to pick out winners,
Trusting performances of the past,
But the dark horse takes first place
While his favorite checks in last!

But surely his luck will change!
So back to the window he goes,
Yet this race proves no better.
It should be the end of his woes.

Then things begin to look up!
He seems to be breaking even --
But desire for more takes over
When he really should be leavin'!

As the day comes to a close
And empty pockets are his due,
You would think he'd had his fill
But tomorrow finds him there, too!

Self Defense

How unjust the accusation
And anger welled up within!
I tried to defend myself
And I know my response was sin.

I should have bridled my rash tongue
But that is so hard to do!
Perhaps the charge was truthful --
I should have considered THEIR view!

If, in fact, I was not guilty,
This, Lord, is all known to You --
So, I can rest in Your mercy,
Who judges what is right and true.

Did I grow from this experience?
Rid my life from fault unknown?
When I can be teachable,
In my Christian walk, I'll have grown!

Serving

I can go to the mission field
'tho my feet never touch foreign soil!
I can visit neighborhood Christ-less homes
and thus for God's Kingdom toil.

A cup of water I can give,
A witness for my Lord can live,
I can speak a word for Him,
bringing light to a world so grim.

As I give of my wealth and pray
and help bear burdens each day
that face those who serve
on a foreign shore.
(I do not feel this time is a chore!)

Their needs for courage, strength
and power
I can bring to God each available hour.
I count it a privilege my prayers to employ
for I'll share in all their triumphs and joy!

The Lord knows each heart, motive and desire.
And so for His approval I daily aspire.
I create my own mission field
whenever my service to Him I yield.

Showing Love

Do you give of yourself to others,
showing love to your sisters and brothers?
Going out of your way,
each and every day --
that the world may know you love God?

Are you quick to forgive, to pardon?
Are you slow to speak words that will harden?
Spreading sunshine and cheer,
quelling sadness and fear --
that the world may know you love God?

Are you patient and kind and humble,
and concerned not to make others stumble?
With a smile on our face,
doubt and gloom do you chase --
that the world may know you love God?

Let no bitterness ever find a foothold,
Let no stranger know poverty or cold,
Let no envy be shown,
let no gossip be sown --
that the world may know you love God.

"By this shall all men know you're my disciples."
They read you like a book, you're my Bibles!
Be watchful what you say,
Be careful what you do --
Let the world see My perfect love in you!

Submission

Can it be that you've lived together this long
And still your marriage is not very strong?
You 'tolerate' each other, yes,
But show little love, you must confess.

You have not learned to listen aright --
It takes so little to cause a fight!
You see "her" as stubborn, as he sees you,
You're both overly sensitive, too.

She picks on your faults and hers are easy to find,
Past offenses so quickly come to mind!
Resentment has built to such a degree
that the other's point of view is hard to see.

It's difficult to talk things out,
for anger soon takes hold,
And nothing can seem to melt
the deep, icy cold!
Your problems you never seem to mend
since neither one seems willing to bend.

You must seek to put one another first!
and not rush to thinking the very worst.
You need to be tender, patient and kind,
no matter how great the disappointment you find.
If you both put the Lord first in your life,
you'll find His answers to marital strife!

Success

How does one spell success?
(A goal that most want to reach!)
Who should know the real meaning?
Whose opinion should we beseech?

How about the COLLEGE GRADUATE,
with his coveted diploma in hand --
countless hours of study behind him,
will he reap a future grand?

Question the wealthy business tycoon,
With possessions too numerous to count --
Does he know a true satisfaction?
Do his troubles diminish or mount?

How about a nation's RULER,
Who such mighty power wields?
Can he rest in peace and comfort
As to strife and confusion he yields?

The PARENT who seeks to raise his brood
To excel in areas he failed --
Will he find they embrace his values,
All mountainous challenges scaled?

(Continued)

How about the world-renowned PREACHER,
Whose influence has traveled abroad?
Will he stand before his Maker some day,
With the approval of His God?

Will the talented ENTERTAINER,
Who draws crowds with worldly pleasure,
Be satisfied with men's applause?
His final worth can we measure?

The ATHLETE who displays exceptional skill,
Conquering distance and time --
Will he retain his strength and respect
When he finds he is past his prime?

No, success is not found
In wealth or power or fame --
It is measured solely by what one does
For God, in the power of Christ's Name!!

The Effects of TV

As a teacher in the public school,
and on Sunday mornings, as well,
I address the watching of TV
and I hope this rings a bell...
One may be glued to every word
or whatever we wish, to ignore.
No-one will ever call us to task
or bar us from heading to the door!
The speaker talking upon the screen
is not offended when we speak --
Is not concerned when we leave the room,
Other tasks and pursuits to seek.

Today's teachers find children "tuned out"
to lessons they try to present,
Kids speak out of turn, devoid of shame,
leaving seats, when not even sent.
It seems respect for authority
is a trait that has gone astray,
And TV helps to erase this grace
as it claims long hours of the day.
TV offers split-second pictures
that stimulate rapt attention --
Teachers must keep their lessons "alive" --
employing clever invention!

And, at home, at the dinner table,
our children are "ruling the roost."
Society is quickly learning...
Interruption of talk we boost!
Fear of adults, at home or away,
is a thing long past, I'm afraid,
Children today challenge one and all,
when parental control doth fade.
Watching TV is good in many ways --
It's educational and fun,
However, the wise will limit time --
to bad habits not to succumb!

The Five-fingered Prayer
Author Unknown

1. Your thumb is nearest you. So begin your prayers
   by praying for THOSE CLOSEST TO YOU.
   They are the easiest to remember. To pray for
   OUR LOVED ONES is,
   as C.S. Lewis once said, a "sweet duty."

2. The next finger is the pointing finger. Pray for
   THOSE WHO TEACH, INSTRUCT AND HEAL
   -- TEACHERS, DOCTORS AND MINISTERS.
   They need support and wisdom in pointing others
   in the right direction. Keep them in your prayers.

3. The next finger is the tallest finger.
   It reminds us of our leaders. Pray for:
   the PRESIDENT, LEADERS IN BUSINESS
   AND INDUSTRY, AND ADMINISTRATORS.
   These people shape our nation and guide
   public opinion. They need God's guidance.

(Continued)

4. The fourth finger is our ring finger.
Surprising to many is the fact that this is our weakest
Finger, as any piano teacher will testify. It should
Remind us to pray for:
THOSE WHO ARE WEAK, IN TROUBLE
OR IN PAIN.
They need your prayers day and night. You
cannot pray too much for them.

5. Lastly comes the little finger --
the smallest finger of all which is where we should
place ourselves in relation to God and others.
As the Bible says, "The least shall be the
greatest among you." Your pinkie should remind you to
PRAY FOR YOURSELF.
By the time you have prayed for the other four
groups, your own needs will be put into proper
perspective and you will be able to pray for
yourself more effectively.

The Marathon Of Life

In the "Marathon of Life" all men are running
And each is striving hard to reach a goal!
Some for riches, fame and pleasure use their cunning,
Not caring that they lose their precious soul.

The pleasures of this world are all so fleeting,
There's not a one that overbooks its stay!
How wise to heed the Son of God, Who's calling,
"Come, follow Me, I AM THE ONLY WAY!"

For what do you profit if you gain the whole world,
The world, with its pomp, will pass away.
The only thing that matters is your name is written down
In the "Lamb's Book of Life" on Judgment Day.

The history of man will soon be ended
But God's Eternal Plan continues on.
When Satan's earthly kingdom is suspended,
The hopes of sinful men will all be gone.

In the "Marathon of Life" all men are running,
And all must cross the finish line some day.
You must lay aside the weights that would beset you
If the words, "Well Done," you'd hear the Master say!

What God Wants You To Know

Please look up these verses in your Bible.
They are many but explain
what God wants you to know!

❧

(1) John 3:16 - God loves YOU!
(2) Romans 3:23 - Everybody has sinned
(3) Romans 6:23 - God MUST punish sin
(4) Romans 6:23 - Salvation is a GIFT
(5) Romans 10:9,10 - You MUST believe in CHRIST
(6) I John 1:7 - Christ's blood cleanses from ALL sin!
(7) I John 5:13 - We CAN KNOW we have
eternal life
(8) Ephesians 2:8 - We are saved by God's
GRACE (His undeserved favor)
(9) Ephesians 2:9, Titus 3:5 - - We are not saved
by our WORKS
(10) Acts 4:12 - No-one but Christ CAN save you
(11) John 14:6 - Jesus is the ONLY way to God
(12) Hebrews 7:22-28 - There is no need for priests
or continual sacrifice today for Jesus'
blood was shed ONCE and FOR ALL!
(13) Romans 10:17 and 15:4 - We learn about God
thru reading the Bible
(14) Romans 10:2 - We can be WRONG in
what we believe!
(15) Romans 5:1,2 - We can have PEACE
with God thru Christ alone
(16) Psalm 86:5 - God hears and answers our
prayers when we pray ONLY to Him
(17) Isaiah 55:6 - We are to seek the Lord and
call on Him
(18) Revelation 22:19 - No one is to add
or take away from God's Word

Who Deserves The Glory?

Can you beautifully sing a song?
Write stirring poems or books?
In sports, are you daring and strong?
Do all admire your good looks?

Been prosperous with business or lands?
You feel you've a right to hold your head high?
Has success rewarded your brilliant plans,
Deserving of praise as a great gal or guy?

WAIT!

LORD, You're the source of all life and breath.
All talents and abilities are from Thee!
All one has is from you, we confess.
This truth let us truthfully, plainly see!

We can't take honor that belongs to God --
Boastful of the things we say or do,
For without Him we truly are nothing --
Without Him, we'd not even have a clue!

ALL glory belongs to our God above,
Who is all wisdom, strength and beauty --
To bring honor to His wonderful Name
Is our humble and thankful duty.

Our Family Prayer

BLESS OUR HOME, DEAR LORD, WE PRAY,

KEEP US SAFE AT WORK AND PLAY.

GUIDE OUR THOUGHTS AND WHAT WE SAY,

YOUR PERFECT WILL WE WILL OBEY.

WHEN WE'RE TROUBLED THROUGH THE DAY,

OUR BURDENS AT YOUR FEET WE'LL LAY.

Epilogue

The writer, either of poem or tale,
Does not always place it for sale.
The expression of each heart-felt thought
Is sometimes too special to be bought.

But, however his works are made public,
He wants them to speak to others,
Hoping they'll be read carefully
And bring fresh blessing to another.

Some works are destined to travel afar
By book, magazine or internet.
Some will challenge, some will inform,
Yet its readers will never be met.

How special it is when someone responds
By e-mail or letter
To let the author knows its truths
Served to help him/her understand better!

Please respond to:

638 S. Hawthorne Av, Elmhurst, IL 60126
or (630) 832-4469
roybet@sbcglobal.net

Alphabetical Index

Abstinence	151
Accidents	24
Adultery	120
Allowance	77
All Of Life	152
Alzheimer's	140
America	124
Angels	134
Anti-christ	145
Appreciation	123
Atheists	138
A Toddler's Prayers	153
Believing	71
Be Involved	155
Bible	66
Big Or Little?	156
Body	84
Catastrophies	107
Children	8
Choices	98
Church	74
Come Sailing With Me!	158
Commitment	119
Competition	89
Comprehending God	159
Computers	102
Consideration	18
Contentment	59
Courting	117
Coveting	83
Creation	132
Dare!	160
Dating	116
Death	141
Deceit	44

Dexterity	48
Diet	40
Diversity	126
Don't Let Go!	161
Do We Think We Know It All?	162
Drinking	52
Dumping!	164
Ears	34
Eating	39
Epilogue	190
Evolution	133
Exercise	85
Eyes	30
Failure	108
Faith	68
Fathers	9
Favoritism	23
Fears	104
Feet	54
Forgiving	29
Friendships	15
Funerals	142
Future	115
Gambling	53
Gifts	81
Giving	64
Goals	105
God	65
God's Agenda	147
God's Ten Commandments	73
God's Will	130
Gossip	45
Grandparents	11
Guidance	114
Hands	47
Happiness	60
Heart	55

Heaven	144
Heroes	92
Holy Spirit	127
Honesty	57
Hope	112
Humility	93
Hygiene	21
Idols	129
Illness	110
Introduction	1
I Don't Want A 'Grumpy' Grandma!	165
I Ran Away From Home!	166
Jealousy	62
Joy!	61
Judging	90
Judgment	146
Knowledge	95
Laziness	20
Listening	35
Looking	31
Love	56
Luxuries	167
Lying	43
Marriage	118
Marriage Is Forever	168
Memorizing	101
Minds	94
Missionaries	131
Mothers	10
Mouths	38
My Car	169
My Prayer	170
My Riches	171
Names	12
Neatness	17
Neighbors	16
Night Light	172

Obedience	13
Obstacles	106
Old Age	139
Our Family Prayer	189
Our Flag	125
Parenthood	7
Patience	28
Paying Attention	173
Play	87
Popularity	91
Prayer	79
Prayer Is...	175
Prayer Project	154
Priorities	99
Promises	46
Protection	113
Punishment	14
Race Track	176
Reading	32
Respect	36
Revenge	26
Saints	128
Salvation	72
Satan	135
Schedule of Future Events	148
Schoolwork	37
Selfishness	63
Self Defense	177
Servants	122
Serving	178
Sharing	22
Showing Love	179
Sin	136
Sleep	86
Smile	41
Smoking	51
Sorrow	109

Sports	88
Stealing	50
Stubbornness	27
Studying	100
Submission	180
Success	181
Suffering	111
Talents	82
Television	33
Temper	25
Temptation	137
Thankfulness	58
The Effects of TV	183
The Five-fingered Prayer	184
The Marathon Of Life	186
The Rapture	143
Thoughts	97
Time	19
Tithing	78
Tongue	42
To Adults	5
To Boys And Girls	3
To Parents	2
To Seniors	6
To Teens	4
Trust	70
Truth	67
Unity	76
What God Wants You To Know	187
Who Deserves The Glory?	188
Wisdom	96
Witnessing	80
Work	121
Works	69
Worry	103
Worship	75
Writing	49

About The Author

ELIZABETH Rosemary Snyder PEARSON
was born in Hanover, Indiana on August 3, 1928,
has three younger siblings:
Albert, Edward and Marjorie.
Al and Betty were heard each Sunday afternoon on
Radio station WMBI as "Billy & Patty Bangle" with
"Aunt Theresa " Worman on "The K.Y.B. (Know
Your Bible Club)" from c.1937-42.

She is the mother of two boys and a girl:
Robert Roy, Phillip Raymond and Cheryl Elizabeth.
Grandmother of five: two girls, three boys --
Kaitlyn Elizabeth, Linnea Elise, Torin Patrick,
Connor Bryan and Andrew Nathaniel,
ages at this writing, 14-18.

Has lived in Elmhurst, Illinois for almost 70
years. Educated at Wheaton College Academy
(Wheaton, IL) Class of 1946. Attended Wheaton
College 3 years (1947-49). Worked as personal
secretary at Sears' Midwest Territorial Office in Chicago.
Married Roy Pearson June 9, 1951 and celebrated
56 years together in 2007.

After 18 years, returned to school to earn a BS degree in
Elementary Education at Elmhurst College (IL) in 1970 and
at age 42, began an 18-year teaching career at Salt Creek
Elementary School in Elmhurst, teaching 3rd (3 yrs), then 2nd
grade (15 yrs). Earned MS from Northern (IL) U. (1978).

For a period of ten years, she had her class build
"egg-carton creations on wooden frames her husband erected.
Included were an Egg-loo, Eggs-change Store, Egg-o-mobile;
Egg Carton Castle, Egg-stra Scoop Newspaper Office,
Egg-spurt Factory, Egg-ceptional Space Capsule,

Eggs-act Copy of Original School Building, Eggs-press
Locamotive (with engine, coalcar and Caboose!)
The most notable one was a replica of the
White House when Reagan became President.
Each student wrote a letter to the president and a photo
that was published in the Chicago Tribune was sent.
The President replied with letters addressed to Betty and her husband
and each student received a booklet about the White House.

Betty (her lifelong nickname) has attended Grace Bible Church
in Elmhurst, IL for 68 years. Has served as Sunday School
teacher and/or Department Superintendent, Vacation Bible
School as : teacher, secretary/treasurer, nurse; Church Secretary,
Treasurer, Editor/Contributor church newsletters: "Grace Notes" &
"Growing in Grace," Nursery attendant, President Ladies
Missionary Society; Choir, Ladies Trio; Drama Team.
Attends weekly prayer meeting & Ladies Bible Study, plans
bulletin boards, member of Community Impact Committee.

Has had over 250 "Letters to the Editor" printed
to The Chicago Tribune, The Daily Herald,
The Doings, The Elmhurst Press and The Independent.

Author of "Points to Ponder – Poetry and Prose to
Challenge the Mind and Heart´-- distributed by
AUTHORHOUSE.com and sold at
Borders, Barnes & Noble and Amazon.

CPSIA information can be obtained at www.ICGtesting.com
Printed in the USA
LVOW12s0000101114

412814LV00001BA/102/P